The Secrets of Strategic Management:

To order additional copies, please contact us.
BookSurge, LLC
www.booksurge.com
1-866-308-6235
orders@booksurge.com

H. IGOR ANSOFF,
PETER H. ANTONIOU

THE SECRETS
OF STRATEGIC
MANAGEMENT:
THE ANSOFFIAN APPROACH

The Ansoff Institute
OPEN Company Ltd.
2005

The Secrets of Strategic Management:

TABLE OF CONTENTS

TABLE OF FIGURES

"THE FAILURE TO CAPITALIZE

ON THE SEA OF CHANGE

IN OUR INDUSTRY IS THE

SINGLE MOST IMPORTANT

MISTAKE IBM HAS MADE

IN THE LAST DECADE"

Lou V. Gerstner Jr. CEO of IBM
New York Times, March 25, 1994

ACKNOWLEDGEMENT

Our thanks to Dr. Pat Sullivan and Katherine Whitman who spent a tremendous amount of time and effort in reviewing and editing the thoughts and content presented in this book. Their resilience in the process sustained us to complete this book. We especially would like to thank; Marcela Enriquez-Pilz and Daniel Macaria for the tremendous amount of work in putting together and organizing drafts of this book; Dr. Alfred Lewis who was the driver in making this manuscript published.

We want to acknowledge the invaluable contribution of all Ansoff Associates who practice the Ansoff methodology around the world namely, Mr. Goran Engberg, OPEN Company Ltd; Mr. Dongjoon Park, Ansoff, Korea; Mr. Ken-Ichi Nakamura, Japan Strategic Management Society; Mr. Seet Seng Pun, Ansoff, Singapore.

Peter H. Antoniou, MIBA, DBA

The Ansoff Institute

OPEN Company Ltd.

2166 Lemon Avenue
Escondido, CA 92029

84 Brook Street
London W1K 5EH

Tel: 760 740 0258
Fax: 760 740 0259
Email: peter.antoniou@opencompany.net
Web Site: www.opencompany.net
www.ansoff.com

WHY YOU SHOULD READ THIS BOOK

Today's market is replete with strategic management books offering different prescriptions for optimizing profitability of business firms. Therefore, it is only fair to inform potential readers about the differences between this book and its numerous competitors.

Each of the competing books offers a success prescription, which is different from all others and claims to optimize profitability of all firms. Use of these solutions in business firms optimizes profitability in some firms and fails to do so in others. Typically authors of the respective prescriptions do not explain the reasons for the failures and successes.

This book differs from its competitors' in the following ways:
- It is based on a Strategic Success Paradigm (SSP) validated in over 1,500 organizations/Strategic Business Units (SBUs) in 8 countries during 20 years of field research.
- It has been successfully applied to SBUs and organizations.
- The Strategic Success Paradigm states that firms succeed when their external strategy and internal capability are both aligned with the turbulence in the firms' environment.
- The Paradigm enables managers to diagnose their firm's readiness to succeed in the future and to develop and implement plans which will optimize their firm's profitability.

THE TARGET AUDIENCE

This book is addressed to a group of readers who want to improve their knowledge of profit optimization in the turbulent environment of the 21st century and beyond.

This group includes:

- CEOs, corporate officers and managers involved in optimizing the profitability of their firms,
- Members of Boards of Directors,
- Thoughtful investors, and
- Students of Strategic Management who want to understand Strategic Management in highly turbulent environments.

CAUTION TO READERS

During the first half of the 20th century most American managers were trained to believe that simple solutions to business problems were the successful solutions, and that complex solutions were suspect.

This conviction worked very well during the first half of the 20th century when the prescription for success was: "make it as simple as possible".

As will be shown in this book, this prescription will become dangerous during the turbulent 21st century when simple responses are guaranteed to fail.

Therefore this book is written on a prescription for success offered by the renowned physicist Albert Einstein. Translated into managerial language this prescription states:

**MAKE THE ORGANIZATION'S RESPONSE
TO THE ENVIRONMENT
AS SIMPLE AS POSSIBLE,
BUT NOT SIMPLER**

Since the business environment of the 21st century is very complex, the readers should be prepared to cope with substantial complexity.

SAMPLE OF KEY TOPICS

- Characteristics Of The Turbulent Environment During The 21st Century
- Strategic Paradigm For Optimizing Organizations' Profitability In Turbulent Environments
- Eliminating Strategic Myopia From Business Firms
- Building Flexible Organizational Capability
- Managing Resistance To Change
- Profile Of A Successful Chief Executive Officer
- Planning In Unpredictable And Surpriseful Environments
- Transforming The Organization
- Strategic Management Of Technology

To: Dorothy (Skip) Ansoff

CHAPTER 1
COMPETING STRATEGIES FOR PROFITABILITY

It is vital to conduct Strategic Development and Profit Optimization
concurrently.
The goal of the strategic development process is to optimize the firm's long-term
profitability.

1.1   Historical Development

During the first half of the 20th century, business firms in the industrialized countries enjoyed growth and profitability that were claimed to have generated more wealth than was accumulated during the prior history of man. This success was widely credited to the *productivity paradigm*, which was proposed in 1776 by English philosopher-economist, Adam Smith. Translated into modern business language, the productivity paradigm stated that the profitability of firms was highest when their workers' productivity was maximized. Adam Smith's paradigm was widely adopted by business firms and was credited for the spectacular growth and profitability of American firms during the first half of the 20th century.

In the United States during the 1960's, and ten to twenty years later in other industrialized countries, the performance of business firms began to slow down. In some firms growth and profitability leveled off or declined. Other firms experienced a paradoxical phenomenon of "profitless prosperity": while growth continued, profitability stagnated or turned into losses. By the 1990's a number of prominent businesses, such as IBM and Apple, were faced with survival crises. Mr. Shapiro, former chairman of the DuPont Company, called the firm's future "a new ball game".

Two groups, each composed of managers, consultants, and academics, emerged offering very different strategies for restoring the profitability of business firms.

The first group argued that declining profitability in firms was due to their neglect of the Adam Smith paradigm. This group recommended restoration of profitability by revitalizing the organization's internal efficiency.

The second group argued that declining growth and profitability occurred in firms that were myopic to the rapidly rising turbulence in their firms' external environment. Subscribing to this view, Mr. Lou Gerstner, Chairman of IBM, made the following observation, "The failure to capitalize on the sea of change in our industry is the single most important mistake IBM has made in the last decade" (New York Times, March 1994). The prescription for success offered by the second group was to focus management attention on the firm's environment and develop timely and effective responses to the environmental trends, threats, and opportunities.

These competing viewpoints—optimizing internal effectiveness, and effectively responding to the external "sea of change" - have continued amongst managers, academics and consultants. The 21st century manager is faced with an apparent dilemma of selecting one approach or another.

1.2   The Dynamics of the Business Firm

Figure 1.1, Model of the Modern Firm, shows that a firm's performance is the result of two interconnecting key processes: near term *profit making*, and long term *strategic development* of future profit potential.

The profit making process consists of manufacturing and marketing products or services of the firm. The goal of this process is to optimize the firm's near term profitability, its operating efficiency.

This process can be divided into two complementary sub-measures:

- Efficiency of the firm's production function, which includes purchasing and production of goods and/or services.
- Effectiveness of the marketing function, which includes promotion, advertising, distribution, sales and after sales service. Marketing effectiveness also includes response to the socio-political rules of the game, which are in effect in the market place.

The goal of the strategic development process is to optimize the firm's long-term profitability, i.e., its strategic effectiveness.

This is achieved through the following steps:

- Identification and selection of attractive markets for the new products/services.

- Creation and/or acquisition of new technologies.
- Invention of new products or services using the new and/or historical technologies of the firm.
- Developing prototypes of products for these markets.
- Transferring the prototypes to the profit making process for manufacturing, distributing and marketing the products.
- Relating the firm to the government, stakeholders, and the public to create a favorable climate for the firm's long-term growth and profitability.

Strategic development takes two forms: incremental and discontinuous. *Incremental development* produces a series of products and or services, which are incrementally superior to the preceding ones. The *discontinuous development* uses novel technologies to create new products and services. For example, replacement of cars driven by internal combustion engines with electrically driven cars.

Figure 1.1   **MODEL OF THE MODERN FIRM**

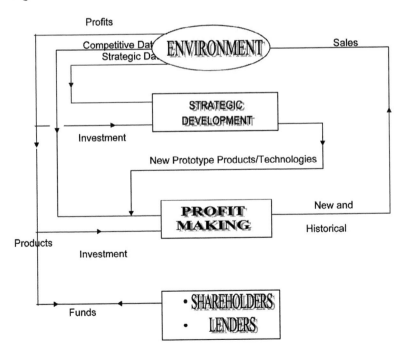

As Figure 1.1 shows, the strategic development and profit making processes are interdependent. The profit making process needs a continual stream of new product prototypes and the appropriate technologies in order to renew the firm's product lines. Strategic development needs profits that are generated by the profit making process for research and development.

In light of this interdependence, some readers may assume that all firms assign equal priorities to strategic development and profit making. However, there is an ongoing struggle for budget funds and power between the Marketing and Production Departments on the one hand, and the Research and Development Department on the other.

This struggle is exacerbated by numerous management consultants and academics who specialize either in *strategic management* or in *profit optimization*, claiming that their technology will solve both strategic and profit making challenges.

As a result, rational managers just entering the 21st Century are left with the dilemma:

Should they put priority on near term optimization, or on long-term profit potential development?

This dilemma will be solved by tracing the relative priorities that were used by successful firms throughout the history of the modern firm. This history is shown in Figure 1.2.

Figure 1.2

ROLES OF STRATEGIC DEVELOPMENT AND PROFIT MAKING

1800-2000

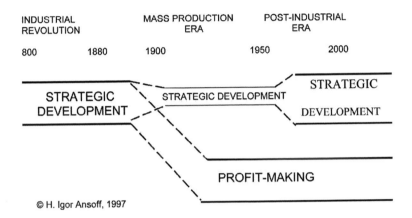

© H. Igor Ansoff, 1997

Figure 1.2 shows that:

- From 1800 until the 1880's, the focus of firms was on strategic development.
- By 1900, strategic development was severely cut back, and organizations shifted the bulk of their resources to near term profit optimization. Strategic development was confined to incremental profit improvement.
- For reasons, which we will discuss later, by 1950, strategic development once again became a major priority of successful firms, but not at the expense of near term profit optimization!

Thus, as Figure 1.2 shows, the dilemma posed on the preceding page is resolved as follows:

1. During the 21st century, strategic development and near term profitability will be equally vital to the success of business firms.

2. Resource allocation between strategic development and near term profitability should be made on the basis of the future

environmental turbulence for strategic development, and on the future competitive intensity in the market place for the near term profit making.

3. It is vital to conduct strategic development and profit optimization concurrently.

The danger of using a sequential approach was demonstrated by Mr. Lou Gerstner's behavior when he assumed the Chairmanship of IBM and publicly declared that IBM did not need a strategic vision and that it must start its recovery by downsizing the firm instead. The result of this decision was a decline of IBM's performance until Mr. Gerstner focused the firm on the "sea of change" in the firm's environment. Fortunately, IBM recovered its position as a leader of its industry. But it is fair to suggest that the recovery might not have occurred in time, except for two factors: Mr. Gerstner's quick recognition of the decisive importance of the strategic "sea of change", and the enormous financial strength of IBM.

Having resolved the dilemma of priorities of strategic development and profit making, the rest of this book is focused on optimization of strategic development during the 21st century.

1.3   Prescriptions for Strategic Success

Between 1965 and the 1990's, academics, consultants and managers invented and offered numerous strategies designed to optimize a firm's profitability during the 21st century. While the proponents of *strategic development* agreed unanimously on its importance, they just as strongly disagreed about the strategies to be adopted. Figure 1.3, Prescriptions for Strategic Success, presents a sample of these various proposed strategies.

Figure 1.3

PRESCRIPTIONS FOR STRATEGIC SUCCESS

- Strategic Planning (Ansoff, 1965)

- Return Back to Basics

- Allow Strategy to Emerge from Functional Levels of Management (Mintzberg)

- Use Logical Incrementalism to Develop Strategy (Quinn)

- "Stick to Historical Strategic Knitting" (Peters and Waterman)

- Build Future Strategy on Firm's Core Competence (Prahalad and Hamel)

- Put Your Customers' Needs First

- Respond to Competitive Forces (Porter)

- No Company is Going to Survive by Virtue of Its History (Kuehler)

- Build the Future on Firm's Historical Strengths

- Use Contingent Strategic Success Paradigm (Ansoff, 1970)

- Competing for the Future (Prahalad)

1.4   Strategic Planning Experience

One of the earlier strategies was developed in 1965 by the senior author of this book. In the book, called *Corporate Strategy*, H. Igor Ansoff presented an elaborate logical process, which he called *strategic planning*, for designing strategy (*Corporate Strategy* by H. Igor Ansoff, McGraw Hill, 1965).

The book, *Corporate Strategy,* received an enthusiastic reception by business firms, and many firms adopted the strategic planning process. It was subsequently translated into seventeen languages.

Several years of experience with strategic planning yielded puzzling and disappointing results:

1   Ansoff's strategic planning did optimize profitability in some organizations, but failed to do so in many others.

2 Use of strategies proposed by others (Figure 1.3) met the same fate; sometimes they worked, sometimes they did not.

3 None of the authors specified the conditions under which their strategies would succeed or fail.

4 Installation of strategies into firms was found to be risky: Many senior executives said, "It is very expensive, disrupts the firm's daily profit making activities, and has a high risk of failure".

This has led to the development of various new ideas by consultants and academics.

Instead of developing non-validated replacements for his original strategic planning technology, Ansoff focused on identifying the variables that determined the success and failure of business firms. He studied the evolution of the firms' environment from the birth of the firm during the 18th century to the beginning of the 21st century. The results and validated support of this study are presented in Chapter 2.

CHAPTER 2
EVOLUTION OF ENVIRONMENTAL TURBULENCE

Firms in the Post-Industrial Era must increase their focus and attention to the multi-faceted strategic challenges of the turbulent environment of the 21st century.

2.1   The Mass Production Era

Between 1900 and 1950 the attention of the business sector in the U.S. was focused on the rapidly growing domestic markets. While growing, export trade was of secondary interest to domestic firms. The trend of economic growth was upward and the profitability of firms was on the rise.

It must of course be noted that this growth was periodically interrupted by economic recessions. But these were relatively short-lived and growth resumed after each one. Even the long economic depression of the 1930's in the U.S. ended with the resumption of vigorous economic growth and profitability.

The business sector of the society, which was creating fabulous national economic growth, demanded and received freedom from government and public interference. "The business of business was business".

The firm's environment during the first half of the 20th century is graphically illustrated in the left-hand side of Figure 2.1, Expansion of the Relevant Environment. The focus of firms was on their domestic customers and competitors, with labor and government receiving secondary attention.

During the mass production era, planning for the future was based on extrapolation of national economic trends and the extrapolation of firms' performance. When firms found themselves in a period of economic downturn, the solution was to cut cost, get rid of "the dead wood", and buy time until "all was well" again.

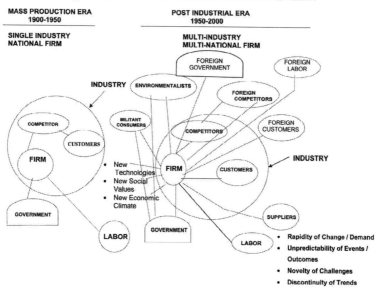

Figure 2.1 **EXPANSION OF THE RELEVANT ENVIRONMENT**

2.2 The Post-Industrial Era

The Post-Industrial Era, which started from the mid 1950's in the U.S., and since then has spread around the world, is highly complex and dynamic. Figure 2.1 compared complexities of the *mass production* and the *post-industrial eras*. The reader can quickly assess the difference between the complexities of the two eras by an eyeball comparison of the left and right hand sides of Figure 2.1.

A somewhat more complex comparison is gained by counting in Figure 2.1 the number of variables which managers must take into account during each year, and dividing the post-industrial count by the mass production count; the results of this calculation produce a ratio of 14 to 4.

The increase in the number of key variables during the post-industrial era puts in question a management principle that was widely and successfully used during the Mass Production Era. This principle states that firms' profitability is maximized when the size of the corporate-level management is "lean and mean".

The large increase in the number of key variables during firms' shift to the post-industrial era strongly suggests that the size of the corporate office should be increased, rather than decreased, to enable the corporate office cope with the increase in general managers' work. This suggestion is supported by the experience of IBM, which was discussed earlier in this book.

The reader will recall that Mr. Gerstner who, on assuming the Chairmanship of IBM, started a major downsizing to increase the firm's operating efficiency. Although this was very much needed, it did not solve IBM's strategic concerns. As a result, he shifted the firm's attention to the environmental "sea of change" and strategically repositioned the firm.

The above discussion leads to the following recommendation: Firms in the process of transition into the *post-industrial era* must increase their focus and attention to the multi-faceted strategic challenges of the turbulent environment of the 21st century.

This can be achieved by acquiring strategic management skills in the Strategic Business Units (SBUs) and at the corporate levels to enable general managers to deal with the new and novel challenges faced in the firm's turbulent business environments.

Figure 2.2 lists the key variables and environmental dynamics that firms will have to manage during the post-industrial era.

Figure 2.2

Key Variables and Dynamics During the Post Industrial Era

Key Variables During the Post Industrial Era

1. High Environmental Complexity
2. Globalization of the Market Place
3. Proliferation of Novel Technologies and Products
4. Destruction of Industries by Novel Technologies
5. Information Explosion
6. Opportunities in China and the Pacific Rim Countries
7. Competition in Domestic Markets from Foreign Products and Technologies
8. National Cultural and Political Barriers to Business in the Global Market Place
9. Opportunities in Emerging Countries

Summary of the Dynamics in the Post-Industrial Environment:

Future:
- Unpredictable
- Complex vs. Complicated

Changes in the Environment
- Frequent
- Fast
- Discontinuous
- Frequent Shifts of Success Strategies

Success Behaviors
- Unstable
- Multiple

Key Variables and Dynamics During the Post Industrial Era

Key Variables During the Post Industrial Era

1. High Environmental Complexity
2. Globalization of the Market Place
3. Proliferation of Novel Technologies and Products
4. Destruction of Industries by Novel Technologies
5. Information Explosion
6. Opportunities in China and the Pacific Rim Countries
7. Competition in Domestic Markets from Foreign Products and Technologies
8. National Cultural and Political Barriers to Business in the Global Market Place
9. Opportunities in Emerging Countries

Summary of the Dynamics in the Post-Industrial Environment:

Future:
- Unpredictable
- Complex vs. Complicated

Changes in the Environment
- Frequent
- Fast
- Discontinuous
- Frequent Shifts of Success Strategies

Success Behaviors
- Unstable
- Multiple

CHAPTER 3
BUSINESS SUCCESS STRATEGIES DURING THE POST-INDUSTRIAL ERA

The environment of the Post-Industrial Era is characterized by frequent shifts of success strategies.

3.1 Five Success Strategies

The preceding Chapter explored the dynamics of the post-industrial environment. In this chapter attention will be turned to the strategies that successful firms should apply during the 21st century.

The solid black lines in Figure 3.1 show five different success strategies that were used by firms in the late 20th century and very probably will continue to be used during the 21st. These strategy types are briefly described below, and their names are entered on the solid horizontal lines in Figure 3.1, Success Strategies.

1. The mass *production driven strategy* focuses firms' attention inside the firm, and optimizes profitability through minimizing production costs and underpricing competition.
2. *Market driven strategy* focuses on responding to the needs of the firms' customers.
3. *Product driven strategy* focuses attention on continual incremental improvement of the firms' products and services.
4. *Environment driven strategy* seeks attractive opportunities in firms' future environment and takes entrepreneurial risks by pursuing them.
5. *Research driven strategy* focuses firms' R&D on developing novel breakthrough products and processes that are ahead of the state of the art.

The research driven strategy is a potential "industry killer", as illustrated by the historical destruction of the vacuum tube industry by the transistor technology and the current replacement of copper communication cable by optical cable and by satellite networks. Another example is the replacement of analog electromagnetic technology by digital technology.

Figure 3.1
TYPES OF SUCCESS STRATEGIES

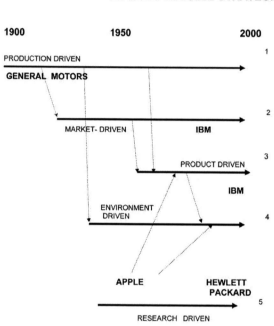

As shown on the top line of Figure 3.1, during the early 1900's organizations used the mass production strategy. As discussed earlier, this strategy was invented by Adam Smith, put into practice by Mr. Henry Ford I, widely adopted by American industry and eventually adopted around the globe.

Also shown in Figure 3.1, at the end of the 1920's some firms began to shift to other strategies. The leader of this shift was Mr. Alfred P. Sloan, Chairman of General Motors, who sensed that the market demand in the automotive industry was becoming differentiated. Mr. Sloan shifted

General Motors from the production driven strategy to the market driven strategy and took leadership of the automotive industry from Mr. Ford.

Another firm to shift to the market driven strategy in the 1960's was IBM, which had established itself as the industry leader by aggressive marketing of its mainframe product line.

As competitors began to offer technologies competitive to IBM's mainframes, IBM shifted to the product driven strategy by progressively improving its mainframe products.

As Figure 3.1 shows, this phase did not last long before IBM shifted to the environment driven strategy. The reasons were twofold:

1. IBM's competitors introduced products to the market that were comparable with the IBM Mainframes, and

2. Advances of software technology opened a fast growing market for computer software products, which redefined the role of the mainframe as a component of computer networks.

It was at this point in time that Mr. Gerstner shifted IBM to the environment driven strategy in the 1990's by making significant investment in software technology in order to round out IBM's position within the data processing industry. Likewise the consulting SBU at IBM received substantial investment in order to attain critical mass.

The Hewlett Packard Company, shown in the right lower part of Figure 3.1, was very successful in pursuing the research driven strategy during the 1940's and 1950's.

In the early 1960's Hewlett Packard became aware that this strategy needed to be replaced by the environment driven strategy. Under the guidance of its two founders, Hewlett Packard planned and executed a successful transformation of the firm's research driven strategy into the environment *driven strategy* and remained one of the top competitors in its industry. The recent HP-Compaq merger is a response to the environmental turbulence.

Apple Computers, founded by the creator of desktop computers, Steve Jobs, provides another example of strategy shifts during the 20th century.

After a period of great success, Apple Computers encountered strong competition from new firms under-pricing Apple. Apple was engaged in two distinctly different business environments: one being the software and the other the hardware personal computer environment. Each environment had different characteristics. Steve Jobs was very good in the software development environment, while the needs of the hardware one were different.

Apple's Board of Directors realized this and hired John Sculley to head the hardware division, a move that surprised many. He was the right person for the level of complexity of the environment of the hardware division at the time, and was hired to strengthen the firm's production management and growth. As the reader might recall, he came from the non-alcoholic beverage industry, which operated in similar levels of complexity, and the success factors were the same.

Due to disagreement about the organization's management, Mr. Jobs resigned, and the reins of the firm were placed in the hands of someone who was very knowledgeable at a level of turbulence appropriate for the hardware division, but not the software environment. Mr. Sculley shifted Apple's strategy to a product driven strategy. The firm's International Marketing Manager, whose focus was also on the product/hardware side, subsequently replaced him. The firm's position continued to falter since software development was in a weakened position. Apple was in dire need of new software development, a business environment with different complexity and demands, and one that the leadership at that time could not foster.

Mr. Jobs was asked to return to Apple, and in January 2000 resumed the title of CEO. He has been revitalizing the firm's software side, adopting a research driven strategy.

A firm that has been successful in adopting the research driven strategy is Intel, with timely product introduction, and clear identification of its customer base. However, Intel is facing some challenges, since the needs of the environment are shifting and the focus is changing.

The above examples show the types of success strategies adopted in the late 20th century and how there were frequent shifts in these strategies.

The preceding part of this book described the environmental challenges that confronted business firms in the past and those they will face in the 21st century. The second part is focused on the responses that firms must make to optimize profitability during the 21st century.

Readers interested in the details of implementing the responses are referred to: *Implanting Strategic Management* by Igor Ansoff and Edward McDonald, Second Edition, Prentice Hall.

CHAPTER 4
STRATEGIC MYOPIA

The first step toward optimizing profitability in turbulent environments is to eliminate a phenomenon called myopia, which blocks organizations from adapting to the environment.

4.1 The Concept of Strategic Myopia

As discussed in Chapter 3, the environment of the *post-industrial era* is characterized by frequent shifts of success strategies (see Figure 3.1). Firms that failed to make a timely response to these shifts also characterize this era. Over time, such failures became frequent enough to prompt Theodore Leavitt to name this phenomenon *"strategic myopia"*. (Footnote: reference to Leavitt's article in HBR)

Giving it a name focused the attention of managers on strategic myopia. However, Leavitt didn't define it, neither did he explain its cause, nor suggest how to eliminate it from business firms.

Strategic myopia refers to managers' inability to see, interpret or predict the firm's business environment, rejecting it as "unrealistic" or "impractical". Myopia might occur due to:
- Lack of appropriate tools to detect change,
- Misinterpretation of signals,
- Organization's arrogance; "we know it all", or
- Unwillingness on the manager's part to accept changes or discontinuities in the environment.

Strategic myopia is the most important element of behavioral resistance to change, because only general management can trigger change to a magnitude that will cause a radical departure from the historical course of action in a firm. In the absence of the trigger, change will be blocked before it starts. Failure to remove myopia leads to lack of response and consequently a drop in profitability, market share loss or other forms of crises.

The irony of strategic myopia is that in the face of a discontinuity from past experience, the most myopic manager is likely to be the one who has been very successful in the past.

4.2 Eliminating Strategic Myopia

In the absence of an explanation, some boards of directors in organizations that were struck by myopia, tried to eliminate it by replacing the firm's Chief Executive Officer. The replacement is usually painful and full of conflict.

In recent years, several methods have been developed and tested, which can help managers avoid myopia. Although different in detail, all of the methods involve helping managers to confront a discontinuous future through guided group problem solving.

The results of replacing CEO's have been mixed. In some firms, the replacement of the CEO restored profitability but has failed to do so for others. For example, Mr. Gerstner was successful by revolutionizing IBM's strategy and moved the firm back to a competitive position in the computer industry. In contrast, Mr. Sculley, who replaced Mr. Jobs at the top of Apple Computers, failed in his efforts to revitalize the firm.

Naturally enough, such discrepancies raised questions about the ability of the CEO to anticipate and eliminate *strategic myopia*. Answers to these questions can be found in rudimentary psychology, which describes individuals by two characteristics: his/her personality profile and her/his life experience.

These characteristics were used to construct three different profiles of CEOs described below: ideal, acceptable and undesirable. The profiles of candidates for CEO positions for organizations in turbulent environments are illustrated in Figure 4.1, Profiles of Candidates for Chief Executive Officer Position for Firms in Turbulent Environments.

Figure 4.1
PROFILES OF CHIEF EXECUTIVE OFFICER CANDIDATES FOR FIRMS IN TURBULENT ENVIRONMENTS

	IDEAL	ACCEPTABLE WITH TRAINING	UNDESIREABLE
PERSONALITY PROFILE	Entrepreneur and Intrapreneur	Entrepreneur and Intrapreneur	Stability Seeking
EXPERIENCE OF CANDIDATE	Turbulent Environment	Extrapolative Environment	Extrapolative Environment

© Ansoff 1992

4.3   Ideal Profile of CEO

The ideal profile depicted in Figure 4.1, describes a CEO who is best qualified to anticipate and eliminate strategic myopia from the firm. The ideal CEO engages in two complementary activities: as an *entrepreneur* and as an *intrapreneur*.

As an entrepreneur the CEO manages the firm by "walking in the future", as compared to the CEO during the mass production era who managed by "walking on the factory floor".

Together with colleagues in the corporate office, the entrepreneur spends a substantial amount of time observing and interpreting early signs of emerging discontinuities in the environment such as impending shifts in success strategies, technological breakthroughs, emerging/declining demand in the market place, demographics, political discontinuities, etc. And, again with his/her colleagues, the CEO formulates the future strategy of the firm.

It should be noted that many current strategic management texts/ books advise top managers to use corporate planners to prepare strategic plans and limit their own participation in planning, examining and approving them. This advice is a leftover from the mass production era, during which most new strategies were extrapolations of the past. Under those conditions, delegation of planning to the corporate staff made some sense. But, during the post-industrial era, delegation of strategic planning becomes dangerous to the firm's survival. Therefore, the corporate office must be prepared to continuously monitor strategic plans.

In turbulent environments, the ideal CEO must also act the role of the intrapreneur, guiding the internal process of converting strategic plans into future profits.

The need for this characteristic of the ideal profile of the CEO was born during the post-industrial era when, in order to succeed in implanting the new strategy, the CEO had to make drastic and frequent shifts in the firm's strategy, encountering strong organizational resistance to changes.

As a result, having conceived the firm's new strategy, the CEO must confront the very difficult task of converting this resistance, at a minimum, into acceptance, and ideally, into an enthusiastic following of the new strategy.

Figure 4.1 also shows that the ideal CEO must have knowledge of managing in turbulent environments. Lacking this experience, a new CEO is likely to make serious mistakes during his/her early days in the office. Mr. Gerstner did make such a mistake during his early days at IBM by focusing on downsizing the firm instead of focusing on the "sea of change".

To summarize, the successful CEO must combine the skills and knowledge both as an entrepreneur and intrapreneur.

As an entrepreneur, the CEO must:
- Continuously monitor the environment for weak signals of emerging new trends, threats, and opportunities,
- Translate them into the new strategy of the firm, and
- Implement the strategy.

As an intrapreneur, the CEO must:
- Anticipate and diagnose the inevitable organizational resistance to change,
- Overcome this resistance to change,
- Inspire fellowship and allegiance,
- Redesign the organization to manage new challenges, and, most importantly,
- Transform the organization's view of the environment from an extrapolation of the past into a creation of a new vision of the future.

4.4 Profile of Candidates Requiring Training for the CEO Position

When ideal candidates are not available to the firm, an alternative choice is described as "acceptable, but requires training" in Figure 4.1. This candidate has the required personality traits, but lacks the necessary experience and exposure to managing in discontinuous environments. Such individuals are typically available among the top functional level managers, such as heads of finance, production, marketing, research and development or SBU managers.

Given their entrepreneurial and intrapreneurial profiles, such managers could quickly acquire experience in managing under turbulence. Two alternatives are available: to appoint such a manager as an understudy to a CEO who is scheduled to retire, or to send him or her to an extensive training course in one of the business schools, specializing in training future CEOs. A lot of firms opt to hire outsides that already possess these skills. Of course there are obvious advantages and disadvantages with this approach.

4.5 Profile of Unacceptable CEO

The last profile in Figure 4.1 is of an unacceptable candidate. The candidate's profile is stability seeking, and the business experience is confined to a stable environment.

Experience shows that such profiles are difficult to convert into risk taking entrepreneurial/intrapreneurial managers.

4.6 Leading a Firm in a Turbulent Environment

The preceding analysis of strategic myopia enables a Board of Directors of a firm to select a CEO who is qualified to lead the firm in turbulent environments, and thus eliminate strategic myopia.

The first step of the new CEO must be to make sure that all managers of the firm understand and share knowledge of the characteristics of the firm's future environment.

The second step by the CEO should be to assure that the firm's organizational structure is fully capable of responding to environmental turbulence, particularly the speed and unpredictability of the environment.

The third step should be to assure that the firm has the tools and know-how to develop the appropriate strategy.

CHAPTER 5
SHIFT FROM EXTRAPOLATION OF THE PAST
TO FOCUS ON THE TURBULENT FUTURE

In turbulent environments, extrapolation of performance by organizational units became unreliable, and...it became necessary to analyze the environment of the firm in terms of distinct areas of trends, threats and opportunities

5.1   Transforming the Organization

In order to succeed, firms need a clear understanding of the structure and dynamics of their environment. As was shown in our discussion of strategic myopia, during the 1880's, many firms had little understanding of the rapidly growing turbulence in their environment.

One such firm was the General Electric Corporation, which was a large and successful firm. It had gained its success by focusing its attention on its historical successes by improving its historical technologies, developing new products based on these technologies, and marketing them to the firm's historical customers as well as introducing new solutions to existing and new customers.

In 1980 the Board of General Electric appointed a new CEO, named Jack Welch. As history has shown, Mr. Welch had an *ideal profile* for success in turbulent environments. This has been shown subsequently by Mr. Welch's performance in General Electric. (To review an *"ideal profile"* see Chapter 4.)

Having worked for General Electric for many years, Mr. Welch was keenly aware that GE was living on borrowed time. Therefore, his first step was to launch a company-wide, vigorous program to align GE with the turbulence of the 21st century environment for each of the firm's *strategic business units* (SBUs). To date, the result of this program has made GE one of the largest and highly successful firms in the world.

Mr. Welch used a variety of approaches to transform GE. Two of these approaches are directly relevant to the subject of this chapter: *'walk the talk'* and *strategic business area (SBA)* based restructuring.

5.2   Walk the Talk

Mr. Welch called the first approach *"walk the talk"*.

Together with his senior managers and managers of the firm's strategic business units, he conducted a series of informal "give and take" group discussions throughout the firm. These discussions were aimed at producing two results:

- To shift GE's energy from a focus on extrapolation of historical successes to identifying and pursuing attractive future opportunities in the environment.
- To gain acceptance throughout the organization for "the firm of the future", GE strategies were developed by the corporate office in conjunction with the heads of strategic business units.

5.3   Restructuring Strategic Management to Face the Future

Mr. Welch's second approach to shifting GE's focus to the future was to redesign strategic planning.

At the time when Mr. Welch became the CEO, GE, like many others, started its *strategic planning cycle* by identifying the firm's historical strengths and weaknesses and developed its Strategic Plan built on strengths and minimized use of weaknesses.

At the launching of his first Strategic Plan, Mr. Welch announced to everyone involved in strategic planning that henceforth strategic planning will start by focusing on identifying the future trends, opportunities, and threats that would confront GE in the long term future.

The idea was to force everyone to interpret the environment with the "outside-in" approach. GE is still following the same approach, forming cross-functional teams making and discarding decisions in a dynamic process. Mr. Welch called the "the boundariless organization" following the thought that ideas should be cross-fertilized across divisions and SBUs.

GE was one of the firms that realized that the environment was getting too complex to be dealt with as a single entity. How it got to that stage is explored next.

5.4   From an "Inside-Out" to an "Outside-in" Shift

In the early approaches to strategy formulation, the first step was to identify "the business that we are in". This reflected the common threads that give the firm coherence and distinctive character, and at the same time, put a boundary around its expansion and diversification ambitions. Thus, Theodore Leavitt, who in the 1960's criticized railroads and petroleum companies for failing to articulate their business concepts, suggested that the former declare themselves to be in the "transportation business" and the latter in the "energy business".

For the early strategists, the definition of "the business we are in" and identification of the firm's strengths and weaknesses constituted the extent of the attention paid to the historical business of the firm.

By the 1960's, a majority of the middle-sized and all large firms had a complex assortment of product-market entries with mixed financial results. Their prospects had become mixed, ranging from excellent to declining. The variance was caused by differences in the stages of demand saturation, in geographic-economic-socio-political environments, in competitive climates, and in the level of technological turbulence.

It became clear that diversification into new fields was not going to solve all the firm's strategic problems, nor take advantage of all its opportunities, because new challenges lay in the firm's historical business areas. As a result, strategic analysis increasingly placed emphasis on the prospects of the firm's historical portfolio of business. The first step in such analysis became, not defining "the business that we are in", but identifying the distinct business of the firm.

To achieve this, management had to make a fundamental change in its outlook. The perspective of many firms had become introverted, "inside-out"; the business prospects were viewed from the eyes of the different organizational units and the historical product lines of the firms. Future prospects were typically determined by extrapolating the historical performance of the firm's divisions.

By the 1970's, a typical division was involved in an array of markets with different prospects and it was not uncommon for several divisions of a firm to serve the same demand area.

5.5 Strategic Business Areas (SBAs) and Strategic Business Units (SBUs)

In turbulent environments, extrapolation of performance by organizational units became unreliable, and, most importantly, failed to provide insights into differences among the future prospects in different parts of the environment. Thus, it became necessary to shift to an "outside-in" perspective; top analyze the environment for the firm in terms of distinct areas of trends, threats and opportunities that are available to the firm, along with anyone else wishing to do business in that segment of the environment.

A unit for such analysis is a *strategic business area* (SBA), a distinct segment of the environment requiring a distinctive business posture, in which the firm does, or may want to do, business.

The following dimensions identify each SBA:
- Geographical area
- Need being served
- Technology/solution to satisfy a specific need
- Customer type

In some instances a channel of distribution is an added dimension of an SBA.

As the first step in strategic analysis, the representative SBAs are identified and analyzed without any reference to the firm's structure or its current position in them. The outcome of such analysis is the future attractiveness of each SBA characterized by its growth and profitability prospects. Any competent competitor, as well as the firm, could take advantage of the prospects of each SBA.

The ultimate use of SBAs is to enable management to make the following key strategic decisions:
- In which SBAs will the firm do business in the future?
- What competitive position will the firm occupy in each SBA?
- What competitive strategy will the firm pursue to gain & maintain this position?

IBM has redesigned its structure based on the SBA approach. Another firm, Ericsson, reorganized and adopted an identical format.

The pioneering work in developing the environment-centered perspective was done by R. McNamara and C.J. Hitch in the US Department of Defense. They developed the "mission slice", which is the military counterpart of an SBA. In business, the pioneer was General Electric, which developed a complementary concept called *strategic business unit* (SBU).

The SBU is a unit of a firm having the responsibility for developing the firm's strategic position in one or more SBAs. The concept of SBA and SBU is illustrated in Figure 5.1, Strategic Segmentation.

Figure 5.1

STRTEGIC SEGMENTATION

SBA is a segment of the environment
SBU is a unit of the firm in charge of one or more SBAs

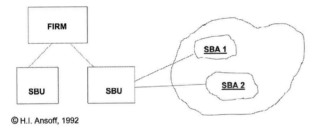

© H.I. Ansoff, 1992

5.6 Strategic Segmentation

When the SBA-SBU approach is first introduced in a firm, an important question is how to structure the SBU/operating unit relationship so that the SBU becomes a true profit center. To avoid duality of responsibilities, GE undertook the difficult task of matching existing operating units to the firm's SBAs, thus making the firm's SBUs responsible, not only for strategy design and implementation, but also for subsequent profit making.

This approach unifies profit and loss (P&L) responsibilities in each SBU. However, GE and other firms that have adopted this approach found that the historical organizational structures do not map simply into the newly defined SBAs and the resulting responsibilities are not clear-cut and unambiguous.

It can be seen from the above that the problem of allocating responsibilities for the firm's SBAs is far from simple, and that the solution will differ from one case to another. Nevertheless, there is enough experience to show that the SBA-SBU concept is a necessary tool for giving an organization a clear view of its future environment, which is essential for effective strategic decisions.

Experience has shown repeatedly that managers have difficulty in segmenting the firm's environment into SBAs. One reason for this is the difficulty in changing an ingrained viewpoint: from viewing the environment from the 'inside-out' view, through the eyes of the firm's traditional product line, to the 'outside-in' perspective, viewing the environment as a field of future needs, which any competitor may choose to address. This is one of the most difficult mind shifts managers face in dealing with the interpretation of the needs of the future environment and its segmentation.

A procedure, which has proved useful, is to ask managers involved in SBA segmentation to avoid using the names or characteristics of the firm's products and focus attention on future threats and opportunities offered by the environment.

At the end of this book there is a list of available tools, one of which deals with how to perform *strategic segmentation* in an organization's environment. Figure 5.2, Logic of SBA Segmentation, shows the four dimensions that describe an SBA, a list of characteristics of performance attainable by successful competitors in the SBA, and the variables which will determine the respective characteristics.

Figure 5.2
Logic of SBA Segmentation

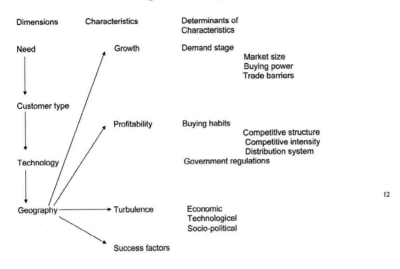

Dimensions   Characteristics   Determinants of
Characteristics

Need   Growth   Demand stage

    Market size
    Buying power
    Trade barriers

Customer type

    Profitability   Buying habits

    Competitive structure
    Competitive intensity
    Distribution system
Technology   Government regulations

Geography   Turbulence   Economic
Technological
Socio-political

Success factors

© H.I. Ansoff, 1984

12

31

CHAPTER 6
STRATEGIC SUCCESS PARADIGM

Appropriate levels of strategic aggressiveness and capability responsiveness to the level of environmental turbulence are required for business success. Significant gaps between appropriate and actual levels would indicate a firm that is poorly prepared to meet the future.

6.1   Setting the Stage- Introducing the Players

Jack Welch, GE, as well as Louis Gerstner, IBM, realized that the environment presented many complexities and a lot of possibilities to their firms. However, they also realized that the environment's complexity and speed of response differed among industries and more importantly different among the SBAs their firms were involved in.

Expanding to a wider range of industries, it is easy to realize that the level of complexity and speed of response needed to operate successfully in an environment varies from industry to industry. For example the environment in the steel industry is different from software development, and they are both different from the golf industry. We are not focusing on the rivalry and intensity within an industry, but on the innovation/introduction of new products/services and the complexity that exists within that industry sector.

The complexity and speed of change of the environment can be measured according to its level of turbulence. Low turbulence represents stable environments; high turbulence represents the faster more complex environments.

6.2   Environmental Turbulence

The level of environmental turbulence describes the types of opportunities/threats/trends in the environment. *Environmental turbulence is a combined measure of the discontinuity or changeability, predictability, and frequency of the shifts of the firm's environment.*

- *Discontinuity, or Changeability* is a combination of the *complexity* of the firm's environment and the *novelty* of the successive challenges that the firm encounters in the environment.
- *Predictability* is similarly described by two variables. The two variables are: *rapidity of change* (the ratio of the speed of evolution of challenges in the environment to the average speed of response in the firm's industry) and *visibility of the future* (measured by the predictability of information about the future, available at the time decision is made).
- *Frequency of Shifts, or Instability* is how often the environment shifts from one level to another.

The levels of *environment turbulence* are illustrated in Figure 6.1, Environmental Turbulence.

Figure 6.1
LEVELS OF ENVIRONMENTAL TURBULENCE

	COMPLEXITY OF ENVIRONMENT	National Economic	→ +	Regional Technological	→ +	Global Socio-Political
DISCONTINUITY	NOVELTY OF CHANGE	None	Incremental Slow	Incremental Fast	Discontinuous Familiar	Discontinuous Novel
UNPREDICTABILITY	RAPIDITY OF CHANGE	Zero	Slower Than Response	Comparable To Response	Faster Than Response	Surpriseful
	VISIBILITY	Total	Extrapolable	Predictable	Partially Predictable	Unpredictable
INSTABILITY	FREQUENCY OF TURBULENCE LEVEL SHIFTS	Very Low	Low	Medium	High	Very High
	TURBULENCE SCALE	1	2	3	4	5

© H.I. Ansoff, 1984

Turbulence Level 1 describes a placid environment in which:
- Firms do business within the limits of their nation state,
- There are no changes in the environment from year to year, and
- The future is expected to replicate the past.

On the other side of the scale, Turbulence Level 5 describes a very dynamic environment in which:

- Firms compete in a strategic business area (SBA) with global competitors,
- There are significant changes in the Environment within a year, where at times, the products/services are significantly different within the same year, and
- The future is expected to be surpriseful and unpredictable and different from the past.

While Turbulence Level 1 is rarely seen in a free market economy, the other levels are all observable today. As turbulence rises, the Environment becomes more complex and unfamiliar, changes become faster relative to the firm's response, and it becomes more difficult to predict future threats, trends, and opportunities in time for an effective response.

Anyone can plot any industry within the turbulence levels. For example:

Tire manufacturer: level 2.8   Biotech: 4.5
Car manufacturer: level 3.2   Health care: 3.5
Rechargeable batteries: 3.5   Digitally produced music: 4

6.3   Organization's Strategic Response

To respond to the environment, organizations have two "tools": *capability* and *strategy*.
- *Capability, or Organizational Responsiveness* is the firm's ability to respond and it includes both the manager's capabilities and those of the organization (system) as a whole.
- *Strategy, or Strategic Aggressiveness* is the firm's application of tools, techniques, and know-how to position itself in the environment.

It is obvious that since there are different types of environments it is necessary to have different sets of *capability-strategy* couplings that are appropriate for each one of the levels of turbulence of environment.

Figure 6.2

MATCHING AGGRESSIVENESS TO TURBULENCE

LEVEL	1	2	3	4	5
ENVIRONMENTAL TURBULENCE	REPETITIVE No Change	EXPANDING Slow Incremental Change	CHANGING Fast Incremental Change	DISCONTINUOUS Discontinuous Predictable Change	SURPRISEFUL Discontinuous Unpredictable Change
AGGRESSIVENESS	STABLE	REACTIVE	ANTICIPATORY	ENTREPRENEUR	CREATIVE
DEGREE OF CHANGE	Zero	Incremental	Incremental	Discontinuous Familiar	Discontinuous Novel
DATA BASE	Historical Precedents	Historical Experience	Extrapolated	Future Opportunities	Creativity

© H. Igor Ansoff, 1984

6.4   Strategic Aggressiveness - Strategy

The Strategic Aggressiveness of the firm's behavior is described by two characteristics:

- The degree of *discontinuity* of the firm's successive strategic moves, such as discontinuity between successive products that the firm introduces to the market.
- The *timeliness* of introduction of the firm's new products/services relative to new products/services that have appeared on the market. Timeliness will range from reactive, to anticipatory, to innovative, to creative.

Figure 6.2, Matching Aggressiveness to Turbulence, describes the appropriate strategic aggressiveness levels that are necessary for success at each turbulence level. Level 1 aggressiveness is rarely observed in the business environment. But it is observed in some not-for-profit organizations that do not change their products/services, unless forced by a threat to their survival.

At Level 2 the environment changes slowly and incrementally, and a firm succeeds if it changes its products only in response to major challenges from competition. In the absence of threats from the competition, such firms do not change their historical products/services. Level Two was typical of the business environment of the first quarter of the 20th century. The great hero of the period was Mr. Henry Ford who "gave (the model T car) to them in any color so long as it was black".

On Level 3 the "heroes" are organizations that continually improve their historical products/services in anticipation of the evolving needs of the customers. The superstars are organizations that discover the secret of shaping and influencing the customer's wants (for example, through artificial obsolescence).

Firms at Level 4 are in an environment that is subject to frequent discontinuities and poor predictability. This is the aggressiveness level at which the firm applies the strategic management tools. The key characteristics of this level are as follows:

- The firm continuously scans its environment in order to identify future economic, competitive, technological, social, and political discontinuities.
- The principle of "sticking to one's strategic knitting" is replaced with "being where the action is". The firm stays in an industry only as long as it expects the prospects to be attractive and its own competitive position to remain viable. When an industry looses attractiveness, or the firm can no longer compete, it exits the industry in a timely manner.
- The firm continually seeks and enters other industries in which the promise is bright and the firm can succeed.
- Thus, the firm continually and thoughtfully repositions its resources from markets that will become unattractive into growing and profitable markets of the future.
- In every industry in which it participates, the successful firm continually reassesses the competitive factors which will bring future success.
- Whenever the firm's historical success strategies do not match the future success factors, the firm either develops new strategies or exits the industry.

The success formula at Level 5 is straightforward: for an organization to remain a technological leader in developing products/services, it must incorporate the cutting edge of innovation and technology.

6.5   Organizational Responsiveness-Capability

Capability, or organizational responsiveness is the manner in which a firm handles change. Responsiveness types, appropriate to success at different Environmental levels, are shown in Figure 6.3, Matching Responsiveness to Turbulence.

Figure 6.3

MATCHING RESPONSIVENESS TO TURBULENCE

LEVEL	1	2	3	4	5
ENVIRONMENTAL TURBULENCE	REPETITIVE No Change	EXPANDING Slow Incremental Change	CHANGING Fast Incremental Change	DISCONTINUOUS Discontinuous Predictable Change	SURPRISEFUL Discontinuous Unpredictable Change
RESPONSIVENESS OF GENERAL MANAGEMENT CAPABILITY Change Management	STABILITY SEEKING Suppresses Change	EFFICIENCY DRIVEN Adapts to Change	MARKET DRIVEN Seeks Familiar Change	ENVIRONMENT DRIVEN Seeks Related Change	ENVIRONMENT CREATING Seeks Novel Change

Copyright H Igor Ansoff, 1984

At Level 1, where the environment is repetitive and the optimal strategic behavior is change *rejecting,* the optimal responsiveness is to suppress strategic change. The organization is highly structured with hierarchical, centralized authority.

At Level 2, the firm is driven by *efficiency and production..* The organization is introverted, focused on internal efficiency and productivity. Little attention is paid to the environment since it is assumed that minimization of costs will automatically assure success in the marketplace. The firm permits strategic change to occur, but only after operating management has failed to meet the firm's goals. The power center is usually in the production function.

At Level 3, successful firms are extroverted and *future oriented*. The focus is on serving the future needs of the firm's historical customers, using the historical strengths of the firm. The word "our" is frequently heard in such firms. You are likely to hear in such firms, "our products", "our technology", and "our customers". The firm's strategic planning is based on extrapolation of historical success strategies. The marketing function typically drives the firm. Hence, the frequent use of the name market-driven to describe such firms.

At Level 4, a distinctive characteristic of a strategic oriented firm is that, unlike the market-driven firm, it has no attachment to prior history but is environment-driven. Future validity of historical success strategies is continually challenged, and so is the future attractiveness of historically attractive markets.

Mr. Jack Welch of GE, which has been one of the most successful environment-driven firms, has succinctly described such behavior. Mr. Welch described GE's strategic planning process as: "Trying to understand where we will sit in tomorrow's world, and not where we hope to sit, assessing where we can be, and then deciding where we want to be".

Unlike other levels of a firm's responsiveness, no single function guides the behavior of an environment-driven firm. Power over strategic activity is exercised by general managers who balance the contribution of the functional areas. This balance is determined by the nature of the future environmental challenges and not by political influence of a single function.

At Level 5 the creative firm seeks to create new environments. A characteristic which distinguishes an environment-creating firm from production, market-driven, and R&D driven firms is its total commitment to creativity. The past is recognized only as something not to be repeated.

Figures 6.1, 6.2 and 6.3 are summarized in Figure 6.4 which shows matching triplets of **Environment** (Environmental Turbulence), **Strategy** (Strategic Aggressiveness), and **Capability Responsiveness** (Responsiveness of Management Capability).

Figure 6.4

MATCHING TURBULENCE/STRATEGY/CAPABILITY

LEVEL	1	2	3	4	5
ENVIRONMENTAL TURBULENCE	REPETITIVE No Change	EXPANDING Slow Incremental Change	CHANGING Fast Incremental Change	DISCONTINUOUS Discontinuous Predictable Change	SURPRISEFUL Discontinuous Unpredictable Change
STRATEGIC AGGRESSIVENESS	STABLE Stable Based on Precedents	REACTIVE Incremental Change Based on Experience	ANTICIPATORY Incremental Change Based on Extrapolation	ENTREPRENEURIAL Discontinuous New Strategies Based on Observable Opportunities	CREATIVE Discontinuous Novel Strategies Based on Creativity
RESPONSIVENESS OF GENERAL MANAGEMENT CAPABILITY	STABILITY SEEKING Rejects Change	EFFICIENCY DRIVEN Adapts to Change	MARKET DRIVEN Seeks Familiar Change	ENVIRONMENT DRIVEN Seeks Related Change	ENVIRONMENT CREATING Seeks Novel Change

© H.I. Ansoff, 1984

6.6   Strategic Diagnosis

Since the present climate of rapid change and frequent discontinuities are likely to persist for the foreseeable future, it is safe to predict that for many firms, the combination of success factors will be shifting more frequently than they did in the past.

Therefore, one of the key tasks facing general management today is to be continuously on the alert for such shifts and to change the firm's behavior in the appropriate manner. This section, introduces a methodology that identifies the strategic behavior, which will make a particular firm successful in the future environment. The methodology enables management to diagnose the gap between the firm's present behaviour and the future desirable success behavior. We shall call this methodology *strategic diagnosis.*

Strategic diagnosis is based on a model of the firm's adaptation to the environment. The model is based on three variables:

- The *environment,* which presents the firm with opportunities and threats,
- The *strategic response,* which the firm uses to capitalize on the opportunities and respond to the threats, and

- The *capability,* which the firm uses to execute the strategic response.

So long as the pattern of trends, threats, and opportunities remains the same, a historically successful combination of strategic response and capability will assure continued success in the future. However, if the Environment is to shift, a new Strategic response and a new Capability must be developed to assure the firm's future success.

Realizing then that there are different types of environments, requiring varied response on the part of the firm, Ansoff hypothesized that to optimize a firm's return on investment (ROI), the following three conditions must be met:

- Aggressiveness of the firm's strategic behavior matches the turbulence of its environment.
- Responsiveness of the firm's capability matches the aggressiveness of its strategy.
- The components of the firm's capability must be supportive of one another.

Before this formula can be applied in practice there must be a specific understanding of the meaning of "environmental turbulence", "strategic aggressiveness", and "capability responsiveness". In addition, instruments have been developed and adopted by organizations, which can be used to diagnose the degree of match or mismatch among these.

6.7   How Does Strategic Diagnosis Work?

To correctly diagnose and assess the SBA and the corresponding unit of the firm responsible for the SBA, an instrument has been developed with approximately 28 attributes to help diagnose the future external environment and the firm's present *strategy* and *capability.*

We can now use Figures 6.1, 6.2 and 6.3 to outline a diagnosis of a firm's current preparedness for the environmental challenges of the future. The results of the diagnosis are illustrated in Figure 6.5.

- Figure 6.1 is used to diagnose the *future turbulence level,* which in Figure 6.5 is shown to be 4.5. The vertical line on the figure connects the *future turbulence* to the *strategic aggressiveness* and *organizational responsiveness* levels that will be necessary for future success.

- Figure 6.2 is used to diagnose the *present strategic aggressiveness,* which in Figure 6.5 is shown to be 3.
- Figure 6.3 is used to diagnose the *present capability responsiveness,* which is shown to be 2.5.

Figure 6.5

STRATEGIC DIAGNOSIS: STRATEGY-CAPABILITY GAPS

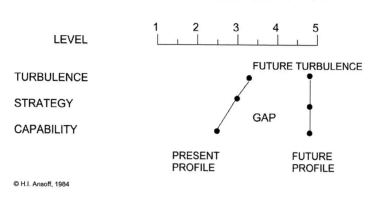

© H.I. Ansoff, 1984

The example of the diagnosis shown in Figure 6.5 shows a firm that is poorly prepared to meet the future. Significant gaps will have to be closed, if the firm is to become a leading competitor in the future.

6.8   Validation of the Paradigm

The Strategic Success Paradigm was a theoretical statement that was proposed by the senior author of this book in 1979. The comparison of strategic behaviors hypothesized in the Paradigm with behaviors observed in practice gives some plausibility to the Paradigm. As its name implies, a hypothesis remains an assumption until validated in business settings.

One way to validate a Paradigm is to apply it in practice. This is a costly and potentially dangerous validation method. If the Paradigm is validated, all goes well. However, if it is not valid, by the time that the lack of the validity becomes apparent, substantial costs will have been incurred, and the success of the firm may have been jeopardized. At the present time the Paradigm has already been adopted by many organizations and has been validated in practice.

At the same time, a less costly and less dangerous approach for testing the Success Paradigm was found. The Strategic Success Paradigm has been empirically tested and validated by doctoral students at the U.S. International University in San Diego/Alliant International University, California, over a period of almost 25 years (1979-2003).

The tests were conducted in a cross-section of industries and in a number of different countries around the world. The list of countries and the results are shown in Figure 6.6. The results of the study of 1056 firms/SBUs with a validity of results of 99.95% or better supports The Paradigm, which says that:

To optimize a firm's ROI both the firm's strategy and its responsiveness must match the turbulence of the environment.

Figure 6.6 illustrates support of Strategic Success Paradigm.

Figure 6.6

STATISTICAL VALIDATION OF THE PARADIGM

1056 Firms/SBUs, p=.05 or Better

United States (Total 234)

- Manufacturing Firms (43)
- Retail and Service Firms (16)
- Federal Service Agency (69)
- Regional Banks in San Diego (15)
- Major U.S. Banks (28)
- Savings and Loan Banks (39)
- California Banks (24)

Japan (Total 475)
- SBUs in Major Diversified Firms

Korea (Total 120)
- Medium Size Business Firms

United Arab Emirates (Total 25)
- Western Banks

Jordan (Total 17)
- Western Banks

Algeria (Total 34)
- State-Owned Enterprises

Indonesia (Total 97)
- Privately-Owned Manufacturing Firms

Ethiopia (Total 54)
State-Owned Manufacturing Firms

Statistical analysis of the data has strongly supported the validity of The Paradigm in predicting the success of firms. What is even more important, the results show that the firm's performance declines rapidly as the Gaps increase.

As shown in Figure 6.7, research conducted on 15 San Diego banks showed that an increase in gap from 0.5 to 1.0 resulted in a reduction of 40% in return on equity. When the gap further increased to 1.5, there was an additional reduction of 20% for a total of 60%. The probability that this finding resulted from chance was less than 0.1%.

Figure 6.7

PERFORMANCE OF 15 BANKS IN SAN DIEGO

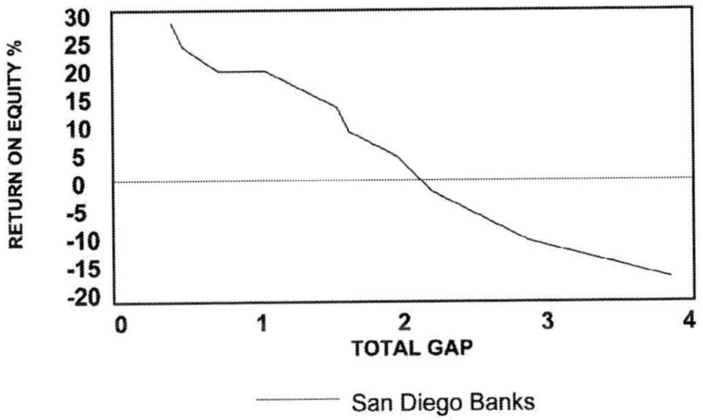

San Diego Banks

© A.O. Lewis, 1989

The results of the empirical research on the Strategic Success Paradigm show that Strategic Diagnosis is a valid practice procedure for diagnosing the type of strategic responsiveness and of organizational responsiveness that a firm needs to optimize its future profitability.

Having such a powerful tool available that can assess an organization's future environment and its current *strategy* and *capability*, led firms to use it as a "physical" to assess where they are in relation to where they need to be. If the firm's *strategy* and *capability* are aligned with the environment, all is well; if not, then changes are warranted.

In addition, the methodology provides a course of corrective actions depending on the attractiveness of the SBA and the size of the *gap*.

6.9   Universality of the Paradigm

The advantage of the paradigm is that it assesses the level of turbulence of the firm's present and future Strategic Business Areas(SBA) and it detects the firm's current abilities.

The paradigm can be used regardless of the type of industry, the product or service the firm produces. It is an umbrella concept, an assessment of any and all industry sectors. Based on the type of environment, the firm can adopt the right strategic response appropriate for the level of turbulence of the environment.

Each of the proposed responses of other authors can be plotted in the paradigm. Figure 6.8 illustrates the position of some of the current popular strategists.

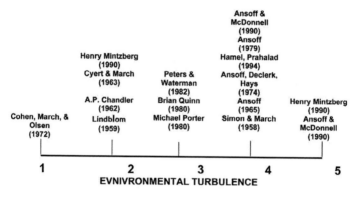

Figure 6.8
TURBULENCE LEVELS ON WHICH AUTHORS' PRESCRIPTIONS OPTIMIZE PROFITABILITY

The major point that needs to be stressed is that every author has a place in responding to the turbulence level of Environment. The proposed responses are optimized within the range of a level of turbulence but not in all. Firms can adopt a Strategy response or a combination based on the level of turbulence their SBUs are operating in and can be successful. When the same strategy is adopted in other levels of turbulence, it will most probably be unsuccessful.

For instance, Figure 6.9 illustrates that the strategies that were introduced earlier can be plotted according to the level of turbulence that are most appropriate.

Figure 6.9

PRESCRIPTIONS FOR SUCCESS STRATEGIES

<u>SUCCESS STRATEGIES</u>	<u>TURBULENCE LEVEL</u>
Strategic Planning (Ansoff 1965)	3
Emerging Strategy (Mintzberg)	2 and 5
Logical Incrementalism (Quinn)	3
Stick to Your Strategic Knitting (Peters and Waterman)	2
Optimize Competitive Strategy (Porter)	3
Return to the Firm's Core Business	?
Optimize Customers' Value	?
Build the Future on Historical Success Strategies	2 and 3
Build the Future on Firms Core Competence (Prahalad)	4
Use Strategic Benchmarking	3
Build Future on Firm's Historical Strengths	3
Use Strategic Diagnosis (Ansoff 1990)	All levels
Use Real Time Strategic Management (Ansoff 1990)	4 and 5

CHAPTER 7
MANAGEMENT CAPABILITY

Management capability design appropriate for expected future
turbulence can be diagnosed by comparing present and future
capability profiles of managers and the management organization
using specific factors

7.1   Concept of General Management Capability

The result of a strategic diagnosis as described in the previous chapter, may show zero gaps between present and required strategy and capability. In this case the firm gets a clean bill of health. It is prepared to meet the future strategic challenges and can focus its attention on profit-making through competitive management.

Or, as in the example shown in Figure 6.5, the firm needs to turn to strategic management in order to assure its future profit potential. It needs to transform its strategy and to redesign its organizational capability. This section deals with the *capability design*. Strategy formulation will be discussed in the following chapters.

Figure 7.1 shows that a firm's overall strategy is determined by a combination of *management* and *functional capabilities*. This chapter discusses *management capability*. *Functional capability* will be discussed in the next chapter in conjunction with *strategic posture planning*.

During the days of management by exception two beliefs were held about general management. The first was that the key general managers constituted the only determinant of management capability. The second belief was that once a candidate was qualified for general management he/she could successfully manage any firm under any circumstances.

As the new concepts of general management evolved, both of these beliefs were increasingly challenged by experience.

The first belief that management capability is exemplified by the key managers remains valid in small firms, where the management group is small and is in direct touch with the "shop floor" workers who develop, produce and market the firm's output.

In medium and large-sized firms however, managers and staff below general managers superimpose a formidable management pyramid between the top of the firm and the "shop floor". If the personnel in the pyramid are unmotivated and/or incapable to implement strategies set by the general managers, the course of the strategies will be distorted or may even remain unimplemented.

Thus, general management capability is determined by two key factors:

- The capabilities of the general managers, and
- The capabilities of the management organization below them.

Each of the two key factors can be subdivided into several components in the manner shown in Figure 7.1.

Figure 7.1

GENERAL MANAGEMENT CAPABILITY

GENERAL MANAGERS	MOTIVATION	VISION MENTALITY ASPIRATIONS AGGRESSIVENESS RISK PROPENSITY
	COMPETENCE	POWER BASE PROBLEM SOLVING LEADERSHIP KNOWLEDGE
MANAGEMENT ORGANIZATION	CLIMATE	VISION CULTURE POWER STURCTURE REWARD & INCENTIVES
	COMPETENCE	SYSTEMS INFORMATION STRUCTURE TECHNOLOGY
	CAPACITY	HEAD COUNT of MANAGEMENT & SUPPORT STAFF

© A.O. Lewis, 2003 (Based on H.I. Ansoff model)

7.2 General Managers' Capability: Motivation and Competence

Figure 7.2 shows the profiles of the influential key managers who are required for successful organizational responsiveness at the respective *turbulence levels.* The top line of Figure 7.2 gives a summary name to the managerial types. The names suggest that different *turbulence levels* require very different types of managers.

Figure 7.2
MANAGER SUCCESS PROFILES

TURBULENCE LEVEL	1	2	3	4	5
MANAGER ARCHETYPES	CUSTODIAN	CONTROLLER	PLANNER	ENTREPRENEUR (INTRAPRENEUR)	CREATOR
Goal	Status Quo	Minimal Cost	Optimal Profit	Optimal Profit Potential	Creation
Success Mindset	Stability	Least Price	Response To Customer	Strategic Positioning	Creative Innovation
Leadership	Political	Rational	Inspirational	Charismatic	Visionary
Problem Solving	Change Control	Diagnostic	Optimizing	Opportunity Finding	Opportunity Creating
				← EXPERTISE IN USING EXPERTS →	
Time Perspective	Past	Present	Extrapolated Future	Predictable Futures	Possible Futures
Acceptance Of Ambiguity	Reject	Tolerate	Accept	Seek	Prefer
Risk Propensity	Suppress	Control	Familiar	New	Novel
Knowledge Base	Internal Politics	Internal Operations	Historical Markets	Global Environment	Emerging Possibilities

© Ansoff & McDonnell, 1990 , pg 174

For example, Mr. Steve Jobs founded the Apple Company, and with it, the personal computer industry, at a time when the demand for personal computers was ready to surface and the technology was ready. It took Mr. Job's creative vision to bring the two together and thus, create a new industry. But, when some fifteen years later the market for personal computers moved from the original creative Turbulence Level 5 to Level 3, Mr. Jobs had neither the motivation nor the competence to change his behaviour from a creator to a growth manager.

It is very significant for discussion to recognize that the person who replaced Mr. Jobs was Mr. Sculley who came from the Pepsi Cola Company whose environment has been at Level 3 for many years.

The above example shows that qualifications needed for general management depend more on the level of turbulence in the firm's environment than on the internal workings of the firm.

7.3   Management Organization Capability: Climate, Competence, and Capacity

Climate: Climate is the organization's propensity to respond in a particular way, for example, to welcome, control or accept change.

Figure 7.3 describes the factors that determine the motivation of an organization to respond to a particular level of turbulence. The generally popular word "culture" is used in a very special sense in Figure 7.3. As used in strategic management, culture is the model of success in the market that is shared by the members of an organization.

Figure 7.3
OPTIMAL CLIMATE PROFILES

TUBULENCE LEVEL	1	2	3	4	5
CLIMATE TYPE	CUSTODIAL	PRODUCTION	MARKETING	STRATEGIC	CREATIVE
CULTURE SUCCESS MODEL	STABILITY	LOW COST	RESPONSE TO NEED	STRATEGIC POSITION	TECHNOLOGICAL LEADERSHIP
NORM	"DON'T ROCK THE BOAT"	"ROLL WITH THE PUNCHES"	"GROW"	"INNOVATE"	"CREATE"
REWARDS	LONGEVITY	COST CONTROL	PROFITABILITY	ENTREPRENEURSHIP	CREATIVITY
FOCUS OF POWER	BUREAUCRACY	PRODUCTION	MARKETING	CORPORATE MANAGEMENT & SBU MANAGERS	RESEARCH AND DEVELOPMENT

© Ansoff & McDonnell, 1990, pg 275

For example, at Level 2, the culture is a shared belief that the market demand is both undifferentiated and highly price sensitive. Therefore; the lowest cost of production enables a firm to minimize its price and thus outsell its competitors.

By contrast, at Level 3 culture is based on a shared belief that demand is differentiated. Thus, success will accrue to the firm that anticipates and serves the needs of its customers through incremental improvement of the firm's products.

As illustrated in Figure 7.3, each model spins off values and norms that encourage behaviour consistent with the model of success.

Thus, the norm at Level 2 "roll with the punches", borrowed from the boxing parlance, means "do not initiate change unless forced by competition". This norm reinforces the Level 2 success model, which depends on repetitive production to minimize costs.

Rewards offer another powerful reinforcement to the success model. Curiously, in current practice rewards are frequently out of tune with the success function which general management is attempting to implant in the firm. For example, many firms that have introduced Level 4 strategic management into the firm continue to use a Level 3 reward system based on historical profitability of the firm, thus providing a powerful *disincentive* to the strategic behaviour needed for success at Level 4.

The above example underlines an important characteristic of the capability profiles. This characteristic is that, for optimal performance, all of the components of a profile must fall into the same column, thus reinforcing one another. Even if the average of the components matches the turbulence level, the overall profile will be *ineffective* if the values of the components differ, and thus work against one another.

Competence Profiles: Figure 7.4 shows the competence profiles of the management organization.

The information component of the competence profile (both formal and informal) provided by the firm's information system is the lifeblood of competence. An information system that extrapolates the firm's past experience at turbulence level 3 at a time when the future is expected to be Level 4, will mislead managers into making wrong decisions. For example, a decision to continue developing improved products at a time when a new technology is likely to make the entire product line of the firm obsolete.

Figure 7.4
OPTIMAL COMPETENCE PROFILES

TURBULENCE LEVEL	1	2	3	4	5
COMPETENCE TYPE	CHANGE CONTROLLING	DIAGNOSTIC	OPTIMIZING	OPPORTUNITY FINDING	CREATIVE
INFORMATION	PRECEDENT	PAST PERFORMANCE	EXTRAPOLATION	PREDICTION	WEAK SIGNALS
MANAGEMENT SYSTEM	PROCEDURES	+ FINANCIAL CONTROL	+EXTRAPOLATIVE STRATEGIC PLANNING	+ENTREPRENEURIAL STRATEGIC PLANNING	+SURPRISE MANAGEMENT
				+ISSUE MANAGEMENT	
STRUCTURE	HIERARCHY	FUNCTIONAL	DIVISIONAL	MATRIX	ADAPTIVE
MANAGEMENT TECHNOLOGY	PROCEDURES	DIAGNOSTIC	OPTIMIZING WHAT IF MODELS	FUTUROLOGY EXPERT MODELS	CREATIVITY

© Ansoff & McDonnell. 1990, pg. 276

Competence profiles become more complex and costlier to develop, as turbulence increases. This is illustrated by the management system component of Competence. As the turbulence level rises, new systems are added to the preceding ones, as indicated by the plus signs in Figure 7.4. Therefore, it is easy to understand the yearning for simplicity and a "return to basics" which many managers experience when their firm's turbulence level moves to a higher level.

Capacity: Management capacity is simply the head count of managers and supporting staff.

As discussed previously, when the environment of most organizations was at level 2, firms ran best when management capacity was reduced to an absolute minimum. And using the maximum decentralization principle was the way to minimize it. In organizations that had previously operated on the maximum decentralization principle, general management could not handle the new workload when turbulence shifted to levels 3 and 4.

A response to this problem was an emergence of the Corporate Office concept that replaced the concept of a single Chief Executive at the top of the firm with group of "nearly coequal" top managers.

Below the corporate level, the concept of a Strategic Business Unit Manager, pioneered by the General Electric Co., emerged to provide capacity for handling the new strategic management workload. A dramatic example of an increase in management capacity is provided by the recent reorganization of IBM and Ericsson.

Thus, at Turbulence Levels above 2, the decentralization principal must be replaced by the "optimum capacity" principle, which assures that the capacity of general management is adequate to handle the environmental challenges.

The curve of optimal management workload capacity at the different turbulence levels is illustrated in Figure 7.5.

Figure 7.5
OPTIMAL MANAGEMENT WORKLOAD CAPACITY

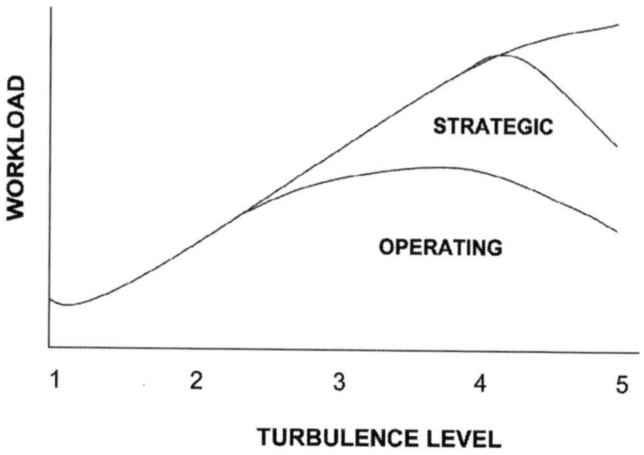

© H. Igor Ansoff, 1984

As the figure shows, up to Level 2, there is no need for strategic activity and the capacity is determined by the operating (competitive) workload. As turbulence rises beyond level 2, additional capacity for strategic workload must be added. At level 4, the optimum capacity curve branches: in firms which are creativity driven the workload decreases, because the firm's strategic thrust is created in the research and development function, and there is less strategic work for general management.

7.4   Designing General Management Capability

The preceding discussion of managers, climate, competence, and capacity profiles, provides instruments that can be used to diagnose the present overall management capability profile of a firm, as well as the needed future capability profile. A summary of Figures 7.2, 7.3 and 7.4 is illustrated in Figure 7.6.

Figure 7.6
OPTIMUM GENERAL MANAGEMENT PROFILES

TUBULENCE	1	2	3	4	5
KEY MANAGERS	Custodian	Controller	Growth Leader	Entrepreneur	Creator
CULTURE	Stability Seeking	Efficiency Seeking	Growth Seeking	Opportunity Seeking	Opportunity Creating
REWARDS FOR	Longevity	Cost Minimization	Profitability	Future Profit Potential	Creativity
PROBLEM SOLVING	Change Control	Diagnostic	Optimizing	Opportunity Finding	Opportunity Creating
KEY MANAGEMENT SYSTEM	Policies	Financial Control	Extrapolative Strategic Planning	Entrepreneurial Strategic Planning	Entrepreneurial Strategic Planning
	Procedures	Budgeting		Strong Signal Issue Management	Weak Signal Issue Management
					Surprise Management
KEY DATA BASE	Precedents	Past Performance	Extrapolation of Past Performance	Vision of the Future	Weak Signals

Copyright H. Igor Ansoff 1992

The procedure is identical to the strategic diagnosis, which has been discussed earlier except that it is confined to the capability diagnosis. An extension of Figures 7.2, 7.3, and 7.4 is used for the diagnosis. The results are illustrated in Figure 7.7.

Figure 7.7
MANAGEMENT CAPABILITY PROFILES

CUSTODIAL PRODUCTION MARKETING STRATEGIC FLEXIBLE

MANAGERS
- Goal
- Mentality
- Leadership
- Problem Solving
- Knowledge

CLIMATE
- Culture
- Rewards
- Power Structure

COMPETENCE
- Information
- Process/Systems
- Structure/Roles
- Technology/Knowledge

CAPACITY
- Line
- Staff

Present

Needed in Five Years

© Ansoff, H. I., 1992.

The next step in the redesign of capability is to identify and implement programs that will close the gaps identified in Figure 7.8. The choice of the future capability depends on the span of the range of expected future turbulence. If the span is narrow enough to point to a particular capability, the choice is easy. If the span is too wide, the solution is to use a gradual step-by-step development of the capability, accompanied by increasing the adaptability of the capabilities.

The above procedures for management capability design have a very important characteristic of the process, which may have remained unnoticed. It is possible, and frequently desirable to design the firm's future management capability before the future strategy has been determined.

This completes the overview of the design of general management capability. An interested reader will find a more detailed discussion in Chapters 3.3 and 3.4 of Implanting Strategic Management (Ansoff and McDonnell, 1992).

CHAPTER 8
STRATEGIC RESPONSE
AT THE BUSINESS UNIT LEVEL

In long-range planning, the future is expected to be an extrapolation of the historical trends. Strategic planning anticipates environmental discontinuities and repositions the firm for success in the future environment.

8.1   A Brief Review

As noted earlier, from the 1960's on, a much more complex concept progressively replaced the historically successful and simple concept of general management by exception. This changed the view of general management's job from a minimal reactive involvement in the work of the firm to an anticipatory and directive involvement.

An examination of the evolution of successful business behaviors confirmed that organizations today exhibit a range of very different success behaviors. It further found that to remain successful in the future, organizations would have to shift their behaviors much more frequently than they did in the past.

As a result, general management must periodically determine whether its historical strategic behaviour will remain successful in the future. Strategic diagnosis has been presented as a tool for such determination. If the diagnosis shows that the historical success behaviour of a firm will not meet the future challenges, the organization will need to redesign its internal capability and develop a new strategic response to the environment.

In the preceding pages the capability redesign has been presented. In the following pages the problem of choosing the firm's strategic response will be explored.

8.2   Evolution of Strategic Positioning Response

Figure 6.1 in Chapter Six shows four characteristics of the environment that determine environmental turbulence: complexity, novelty of change (or familiarity of events), rapidity of change, and visibility of the future. These determinants were grouped into three categories:

1. *Changeability of* the environment determined by a combination of complexity and familiarity (or novelty),

2. *Unpredictability of* the environment, determined by the rapidity of change and visibility of the future, and

3. *Frequency of Shifts* of the environment, determined by its shift frequency from one level to another.

When changeability, predictability and shifts ratings of the future environment are at Level 1 or 2, the optimum Strategic response is very simple. At Level 1, successful behaviour is achieved when the organization continues to produce its historical goods/services. In other words, Strategic response is zero.

At Level 2, changes in products/services are infrequent because optimum performance is also attained through abstaining from strategic change. But aggressive competitors periodically force the firm to modify its products or services.

Over the years, at each level of turbulence, business firms have developed appropriate systematic problem solving procedures, which are called management systems. The system for Level 1 is called procedures (or systems and procedures) and at Level 2 the financial control system. Both systems are reactive in the sense that they respond, after the fact, to deficiencies or deviations in a firm's performance, and both systems support competitive behaviour of the organization.

When the environment moves to level 3, firms have to shift from reaction to anticipation in order to deal with the accelerated changeability of the environment. Progressive organizations at this level invented a new forward-looking system named "long-range planning".

The long-range planning system is built on the assumption that the future environment will be a logical extrapolation of the past. Therefore, the historical logic of product and market evolution will remain the success logic in the future. This type of strategic response was named "logical incrementalism" by Brian Quinn and "sticking to (historical) strategic knitting" by Peters and Waterman. The logic that underlies the evolution of a firm's strategic response was named "strategy" by Henry Mintzberg.

The next and major change in the firm's strategic response occurs when, in a number of industries, the changeability of the environment moves from extrapolable to discontinuous (from Level 3 to 4). It is no longer safe to assume that the future environment will be an extrapolation of the past, and, therefore, historically successful strategies could not be relied upon to be successful in the future.

Again, leading business firms invented a new system called "strategic planning", which is focused on selecting new strategies for the future and redirecting the firm's energies and resources to follow the logic of the new strategy development.

Strategic planning:
- Predicts the future discontinuities in the environmental trends using techniques different from extrapolation,
- estimates the threats and opportunities for the firm derived from the discontinuities presented by the environment,
- develops strategies which will enable the firm to take advantage of the opportunities and avoid the threats, and
- allocates financial and other resources in the pursuit of the strategies

Thus, Strategic Planning repositions the firm for success in the future environment.

8.3   Evolution of Real Time Strategic Responses

In the 1970's, the level of environmental turbulence increased significantly due to the emergence of a global marketplace, the entry of new competitors in the market, the acceleration of technological progress, the growing importance and instability of the firm's socio-political environment, levels of changeability and unpredictability.

As the turbulence level moves from level 4 to 5, forward looking strategic planning is no longer sufficient to assure a timely response to future turbulence. The reason is that the high speed of change and the visibility of the future create a situation in which major discontinuities can surface and impact on the organization before strategic planning can determine effective response.

A complementary type of strategic response has been developed by business firms. The new response does not attempt to develop a comprehensive strategy for guiding the future evolution of the firm. Instead, it seeks to anticipate surpriseful discontinuities one at a time, and to respond to them quickly and effectively. The public utilities industry in the U.S. became a pioneer and committed user of this response. The trigger was the failure of the industry to anticipate and respond to the socio-political pressures against the use of atomic energy in the U.S..

To borrow from computer terminology, while strategic planning is an "off-line" positioning of the firm, the new approach is an "on-line" or "real time" response to surpriseful threats and opportunities. The name of this new response is *issue management*. The word "issue" describes an event that has a potentially significant impact on the firm. Thus, an issue is either a major threat or a major opportunity.

Issue management is responsive to fast developing threats or opportunities, which can be predicted in time to enable the firm to make a timely response. But, issue management begins to fail as environmental turbulence approaches Level 5, at which, in spite of the organization's best efforts, unpredictable surprises may strike the organization. For example, the Tylenol crisis that struck Johnson and Johnson.

Until recently, organizations paid little attention to such unpredictable surprises. But, in the late 1980's, a growing number of organizations began to prepare themselves to cope with unpredictable surprises. This new type of strategic response is called *surprise management* or *crisis management*.

To summarize, since the 1940's, two different types of strategic response systems have been derived and increasingly adopted by business firms:

- The *positioning strategic response,* which includes long-range planning (appropriate at Level 3) and strategic management planning (necessary at Level 4 and above).
- The *real time response,* which includes issue management (for Levels 4 and above) and surprise management (at Level 5).

In the following pages, there is a brief description of the *positioning response systems*. The *real time response* system is introduced separately in Chapter 10, since it only applies in Turbulence Levels 4 and 5.

8.4 Long-Range Planning: Business Level Strategy at Turbulence Levels 1- 3

The basic difference between *long-range planning* and *strategic planning* lies in their respective views of the future.

In *long-range planning*, the future is expected to be an extrapolation of the historical trends. General management usually assumes that the historical performance of the firm can be improved in the future, and negotiates future goals with lower level managers. Typically goals are set through negotiations in which general management proposes high goals and lower level managers argue that the goals are unrealistically high. If the general management is aggressive, the high goals are set. This is the effect that Mr. Jack Welch of GE referred to when he talked about budget/resource allocation fighting.

Once the corporate goals are set, the next step in long-range planning is to formulate goals and programs for each unit of the firm, and to prepare the necessary budgets. The unit goals, programs and budgets are reviewed and approved by general management, and implementation starts. The issue of resistance to change emerges at this point.

Figure 8.1 presents a schematic diagram of the overall management process based on long range planning.

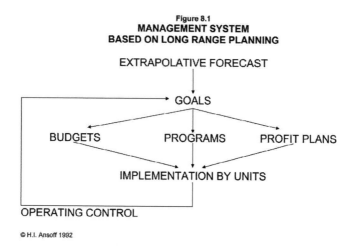

Figure 8.1
MANAGEMENT SYSTEM
BASED ON LONG RANGE PLANNING

EXTRAPOLATIVE FORECAST

GOALS

BUDGETS   PROGRAMS   PROFIT PLANS

IMPLEMENTATION BY UNITS

OPERATING CONTROL

© H.I. Ansoff 1992

The process appears simple and straightforward. In reality, it is far from simple. The reason is that all operating units must participate in the process, requiring both lateral and vertical coordination and integration. Furthermore, the process flows two ways: first, "top down" from general management to the lower units of the firm, and second, "bottom up" from the units back to the general management. As a result, a complete planning cycle in middle or large sized firms can take 5 to 7 months.

The version of long-range planning discussed above is observable in firms where corporate management plays directive and motivating roles. In a firm in which the corporate office manages by exception, the process becomes simpler. It is typically from the bottom up, and, as long as the consolidated goals of the lower units satisfy the corporate management, they become the corporate goals of the firm.

As discussed previously, long-range planning assumes that the historical success strategies are expected to be successful in the future. Therefore, so long as the firm's strategy continues to bring satisfactory results, long-range planning does not concern itself either with changing strategy, or even making the strategy explicit. The initiative for initiating and developing new products and markets rests with the functional units of the firm, specifically the R & D and marketing departments. Development decisions are made at the general management level to which the functions report (e.g. at the divisional level in divisionally structured firms). Corporate management gets involved in strategic development in exceptional cases in which strategic moves require a large scale commitment of resources, particularly plant and equipment investments.

Characteristically, products and services developed within the long range planning framework are incremental improvements on historical ones. Proposals for discontinuous product lines are usually rejected either by functional managers or by general managers to whom they report. It is only when the historical strategy consistently fails to meet the goals of the firm that attention turns to revising the historical strategy. In long-range planning the new strategy is sought among strategies of the firm's competitors who have been top performers in the marketplace. The responsibility for finding the new strategy remains at the lower general management levels.

To summarize, long-range planning is focused on optimizing competitive behaviour based on historically success strategies. Attention turns to new strategies only when historical strategies repeatedly fail to meet the firm's goals. Even then, strategy revision is handled locally in the part of the firm that has encountered a problem with its strategy.

So long as the turbulence level remains at Levels 1 and 2, long-range planning has proven to be a successful instrument, to general management. At level 3, the rapidity of change is faster than the firm's response. As a result, a reactive response is likely to develop a new strategy just in time for the next strategy revision! When this happens, the firm has insufficient time to implement and use a new strategy to recover the investment in its development. That is why firms adopt anticipatory strategic management and control tools.

A big change occurs when turbulence rises to Level 4. The environment at turbulence Level 4 is discontinuous and not extrapolative thereby making reactive strategic management techniques ineffective due to the speed and types of changes. Recognition of this problem led progressive firms to develop an approach for anticipating environmental discontinuities and choosing and implementing new strategies in advance of the occurrence of the discontinuities, thus making the firm's response both timely and effective. Such an approach has been named strategic planning.

8.5   The Original Concept of Strategic Planning

From the mid 1950's on, as the turbulence level moved toward Level 4, firms increasingly found that reliance on historically successful strategies became ineffective. Such firms increasingly encountered slowdowns in growth and decline in profitability, or became vulnerable to the cyclical nature of their business. Firms in the defense industry, for example, became vulnerable to the vagaries of the defense procurement process.

From a historical perspective, it is interesting to note that most firms sought a strategic remedy for their problems by externalizing them. Rather than adopting novel strategies in their historical businesses, firms turned to diversification into other industries. As a result, the original concept of strategic planning was invented to help firms formulate a promising diversification strategy. A skeleton diagram of this concept is shown in Figure 8.2.

Figure 8.2
THE ORIGINAL CONCEPT OF STRATEGIC PLANNING

ENVIRONMENT
(WHAT IS POSSIBLE)

OBJECTIVES
STRENGTHS/WEAKNESSES
(WHAT WE WANT)   (WHAT WE ARE ABLE TO DO)

STRATEGY
(WHAT WE WILL DO)

"THE BUSINESS WE ARE IN"

© H.I. Ansoff 1992

As the figure shows, three basic factors determined a firm's strategy:
- the merger acquisition opportunities available in the environment,
- the objectives and goals of the firm, and
- its historical strengths and weaknesses.

Opportunities were judged to be attractive in proportion to the extent to which they contributed to the firm's objectives and were compatible with the strengths of the firm. As. the figure shows, the strategy was typically a statement of "the business we want to be in" and this strategy guided the firm's search for merger and acquisition candidates. The analytic technology of- strategic planning was rudimentary. Strategic plans looked like essays made up of strategic generalities, which were difficult to apply.

8.6 Strategic Posture Planning: Business Level Strategy at Turbulence Levels 4—5

Since the 1960's, the concept of strategic planning has undergone major changes and the analytic technology has been vastly improved.

Today, a variety of strategic planning approaches can be observed in practice. In this section, the discussion will be limited to sketching the characteristics of an advanced state of the art approach called strategic posture planning. In order to apply this approach, *strategic diagnosis* is used to identify the gap between the present and future profiles of strategy and capability, and the level of turbulence in the environment. (See Chapter 6.)

A major difference of strategic posturing planning from the original concept of strategic planning is that, today, the strategic problems of the firm are no longer externalized. The planning process is concerned both with developing new strategies for the firm's historical business, and for new business which the firm is going to enter or leave.

As a result, modern strategic planning answers two complementary questions:

1. How will the firm succeed in the future in each of its historical businesses?

2. How will the portfolio of the firm's businesses evolve over time?

In the original concept of strategic planning, the firm's historical strengths/weaknesses were expected to remain valid in the future. This expectation is valid in environments at Level 3. But, at Level 4 and above, historical strengths may become future weaknesses and weaknesses may become strengths. Furthermore, if the strategic diagnosis predicts that the future level of turbulence will be different from the historical one, the entire successful historical capability profile will become a weakness in the future environment.

As a result, at Levels 4 and 5, and in environments in which a shift (up or down) of turbulence is expected, strategy is only one of the factors, which determine the success of the firm. The firm's functional capability is another and equally important factor. The third factor is the *strategic investment*, which is the firm's commitment to the development of the new strategy and capability. We shall refer to the combination of strategy, functional capability and strategic investment as the *competitive position* of a firm.

The *competitive position* of the firm in a strategic business area is the answer to the question, "How will the firm succeed in the future in each of its historical businesses?" The *portfolio posture* is the answer to the question, "How will the firm's portfolio develop over time?", which is the historical question, "What business are we in?"

In this and the next section we will discuss how the two types of posture—*competitive position* and *portfolio posture*—are identified. We start with the *competitive position*.

8.7 Competitive Position

Figure 8.3 shows the three components of a competitive position - strategy, capability, and strategic investment. A further breakdown of each component is also shown.

Figure 8.3
COMPETITIVE POSITION IN AN SBA

STRATEGY: **Growth Thrust (Direction)**
                                Market Position
    COMPETITIVE_____ **Market Differentiation**
    NICHE   **Product Differentiation**

CAPABILITY: **Management**
                                  Finance
                                  Marketing
                                  R & D
                                  Production

STRATEGIC
INVESTMENT: **In Strategy**
                                In Capability
                                In Facilities

POSTURE = S*C*(I-Icr)

© H.I. Ansoff 1992

The last line of Figure 8.3 shows an important characteristic of competitive position: the success of a posture is determined by a multiplicative relation among its principal components. This is another way of saying that the overall posture is no better than its weakest component. For example, an excellent strategy without the necessary supporting capability will not be successful no matter how much money the firm invests in development.

By contrast, strategic investment is a relatively new concept to many business firms. A breakdown of the strategic investment components is shown in Figure 8.4.

Figure 8.4

STRATEGIC INVESTMENT IN AN SBA

STRATEGIC INVESTMENT =

STRATEGY   +   CAPABILITY   +   FIXED ASSETS

STRATEGY	CAPABILITY	FIXED ASSETS
R & D	Personnel Acquisition	Plant
Market Research	Personnel Training	Distribution Facilities
Market Testing	Management Training	Machinery
Launching	Working Capital	Other Equipment

© H.I. Ansoff 1992

Strategy is subdivided into five sub strategies, which may or may not be important in an SBA. For example, as discussed earlier, during the first half of the 20th century, most industries enjoyed healthy growth, and choosing the firm's growth thrust was not a concern to managers. But, during the second half of the 20th century many industries reached saturation and firms that wanted to continue growing had to select and execute a specific growth *thrust sub-strategy*. Some chose diversification(related/unrelated), others chose acquisition of competitors, while others rounded out their product lines.

While growth thrust was not important during the first half century, the maximization of market share was the key success sub strategy. Products were undifferentiated and product price was the key determinant of success.

During the latter half of the 20th century, two additional sub-strategies became important:
- *Product differentiation*, the firm's sub strategy for making its products superior to its competitors' products; and
- *Market differentiation*, the way a firm differentiates customers' perception of its products.

Together, they have been named the firm's *market niche*.

As discussed previously, in turbulent environments, the relative importance of the respective strategy components to success, changes over time, as customer needs and preferences change, as technology evolves, and as new competitors enter the market. Therefore, the strategy formulation process consists of predicting the combinations of sub strategies that will be key to success in the future and choosing the success combination that best fits the firm.

8.8   Competitive Posture Planning (Portfolio Posture)

In this section, we will briefly discuss the process of selecting a firm's optimal posture in a strategic business area.

The first step in competitive posture planning is to segment the firm's environment into distinctive areas of opportunity measured by growth, opportunity, turbulence, and distinctive success factors. Such areas are called Strategic Business Areas (SBA). Figure 8.5 illustrates a firm that has three SBAs.

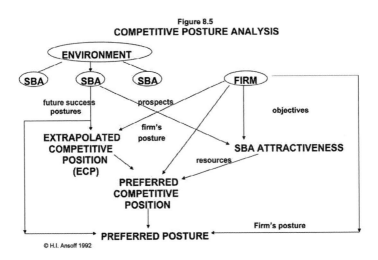

Figure 8.5
COMPETITIVE POSTURE ANALYSIS

© H.I. Ansoff 1992

The second step is to determine the future attractiveness of each SBA to the firm. As the figure illustrates, attractiveness is determined by estimating the extent to which the firm's objectives (e.g. for growth, profitability, strategic vulnerability) will be met by the prospects that the SBA will offer to successful competitors.

The third step is to determine the Extrapolated Competitive Posture (ECP) which the firm will occupy in the SBA if it continues to use its historical competitive posture. As the figure shows, ECP is obtained by evaluating how close the firm's present competitive posture is going to be to the postures which are expected to be successful in the SBA.

The fourth step is to compare the attractiveness to the ECP in order to decide what relative competitive position the firm will seek to occupy in the SBA.

A number of years ago, Mr. Bruce Henderson, founder of the Boston Consulting Group, developed a graphical presentation that facilitates this decision. The presentation became widely known as the Boston Consulting Matrix. A modern version of the Matrix (generally credited to the McKinsey Consulting Co.) is shown in Figure 8.6.

Figure 8.6

POSITIONING MATRIX
Turbulence Levels 1-3

		GOOD	POOR
FUTURE ATTRACTIVENESS OF SBA	**GOOD**	**OPTIMIZE** Stars	**UPGRADE OR MAINTAIN?** Wildcats
	POOR	**MILK** Cash Cows	**DIVEST** Dogs

FIRM'S EXTRAPOLATED COMPETITIVE POSITION

Adapted from the Boston Consulting & McKinsey Consulting Co.

The firm's SBAs are sorted into two categories according to their attractiveness: good or poor. Similarly, the ECPs of the firm in the SBAs are sorted into good or poor. Then, each SBA is entered into one of the four boxes in Figure 8.6.

SBAs that fall into the lower right quadrant have poor attractiveness and the firm's ECP in them will also be poor. Mr. Henderson called such SBAs "dogs" and suggested that management should divest them.

The "star" SBAs in the upper left quadrant are the opposite of "dogs": their attractiveness is good and so is the firm's future ECP. Management should maintain the historical posture and should support these SBAs with resources necessary to assure continued success.

SBAs in the lower left quadrant have poor prospects but the firm's

ECP will be good. The advice to management is to maintain the historical posture, to control new investment in these SBAs and milk them for cash, which is to be used to support the "stars" as well as "wildcats".

As the reader will have noticed, no further competitive posture analysis is necessary for "stars", "cash cows", and "dogs". The competitive posture in the first two is to be maintained, and the "dogs" are to be divested. Therefore, it is the remaining "wildcats" which become the focus of further competitive analysis.

A "wildcat" is an SBA that has good attractiveness, but the firm's extrapolated competitive position is poor. The decision on whether to move the SBU/firm to a "star" position should be based on several considerations:

- Does the firm have the necessary resources?
- Is there enough time to catch up with the leaders in the SBA?
- Is there room in the SBA for another major competitor?
- Will the firm's profitability in the SBA be sufficiently improved to make the effort to become a star?

If the decision is to retain the present posture or to divest from a "wildcat", competitive analysis stops. If the decision is to move to the "star" position, the next and final step in competitive analysis is to choose the competitive posture that the firm will build in order to attain the preferred competitive position.

The choice is comparatively easy to make, because most of the relevant data will have been developed in the preceding stages of competitive analysis.

During determination of the ECP (Figure 8.5) three of four postures will have been constructed which are likely to be the most successful in the SBA in the future. These are now compared to the firm's present posture, and the success posture that requires the least investment by the firm is the optimum future posture for the firm, if it seeks to become a top competitor. If the firm seeks a more modest competitive position, the optimum posture is scaled down to a less ambitious level, which is sufficient to attain the desired position.

As the reader will readily perceive, the preceding discussion of competitive posture formulation is simplified for the purposes of this brief exposition.

Business reality is too complex to categorize a firm's SBAs in four archetypal categories. Therefore, in practical applications, the "good"/"poor" ratings of attractiveness are replaced by scales of 1 to 10. Furthermore, at Turbulence Level 4, future uncertainty is usually too great to permit single value estimates of both the future ECP and attractiveness. Therefore, ranges of probable estimates are used in practical applications to describe ECP and attractiveness. The GE/McKinsey nine cell matrix, illustrated in Figure 8.7 makes an attempt towards this direction.

Figure 8.7

THE INDUSTRY ATTRACTIVENESS/BUSINESS STRENGTH MATRIX

GE/McKinsey Nine-Cell Matrix

As a result of all these refinements, competitive posture analysis in turbulent environments becomes complex and protracted. An interactive computer program has been designed which handles much of the complexity and permits managers to focus their attention on making the key decisions (for detailed discussion refer to Implanting Strategic Management).

The reader is invited to compare the rather complex process of competitive posture analysis discussed above with the considerably simpler process, appropriate at Level 3, of choosing one of the historically successful strategies.

A conclusion is inevitable that the competitive posture analysis of an SBA should be undertaken only if management is convinced that reliance on extrapolation of past trends is dangerous. This conclusion reinforces the need for a thorough strategic diagnosis of each SBA before a competitive posture analysis is undertaken.

CHAPTER 9
STRATEGIC RESPONSE AT THE CORPORATE
LEVEL

The positioning strategic response is in two parts: planning the competitive posture for each SBA of the firm, and integrating the competitive postures into the overall strategic posture.

9.1   Managing Strategic Portfolios

In a modern strategic planning system, Strategic Business Unit managers prepare competitive posture plans for each of the SBAs for which they are responsible. The next step is to submit this plan for approval to the top management of the firm. The concern in this section is with the different ways in which the corporate managers handle this approval. Current practice shows three different methods:
1. Management by exception
2. Portfolio balancing
3. Portfolio optimization

Management by Exception:

The corporate management focuses attention on the budget requests in the competitive posture plans. The budgets are examined, amended and approved. The changes in the budgets requested by the SBU managers are determined by two considerations. The first is the total budget that the corporate management intends to allocate to the firm's strategic development. The second is the firm's historical performance in the SBA: high performers get preference and low performers get the residue.

The remainder of the SBA plans - the strategies and capabilities - are not examined in any depth. Thus, under management by exception SBU managers have the de-facto authority for determining strategy.

Portfolio Balancing:

Rather than reward historical performance, budgeting decisions are based on the future performance promised by the respective SBA plans.

The Boston/McKinsey type matrices are frequently used as a tool in portfolio balancing. All of the SBAs are entered into the matrix, thus providing a picture of the entire firm on a single sheet of paper. The budget requests of the "stars" are approved. The proposed plans for promotion of the "wildcats" are carefully examined and sound plans are allocated the requested budgets. SBU managers are told to divest from their "dogs". Finally, corporate management specifies the cash flow contribution it will expect from the "cash cows".

As in management by exception, corporate management does not concern itself with the shape of the total SBA portfolio. This is not to say that firms which use budget balancing do not engage in diversification of the SBA portfolio. But, diversification is an ad hoc activity, and not a part of the strategic planning cycle.

9.2   Portfolio Optimization

The third method that can be employed by corporate management to handle approvals for competitive posture plans is portfolio optimization. In this role, corporate management is an active guiding contributor to the firm's strategic development process. This role is described below and illustrated in Figure 9.1.

1. The corporate office starts the process by issuing strategic guidelines to managers of the Strategic Business Units (SBU). The guidelines designate the strategic mission scope within which SBU managers will develop their SBAs, propose objectives for the SBUs, and assign corporate issues, which SBU managers are asked to resolve. (See Strategic Issue Management in Section 8.3.)

2. The SBU managers and their staff develop plans for the competitive posture in each of their SBAs.

3. Corporate management evaluates the plans and optimizes the SBA portfolio. (This process is discussed later in Section 9.7)

4. If the resulting portfolio posture calls for diversification of the portfolio, the corporate office assigns implementation responsibilities for some of the diversification moves (such as divestment from SBAs) to the SBU managers, and assumes responsibility for other moves, such as diversifying into industries new to the firm.

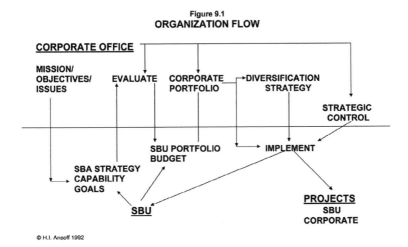

Figure 9.1
ORGANIZATION FLOW

© H.I. Ansoff 1992

In large firms in which there is a Group Level of general management, Group Managers perform an intermediate portfolio optimization for the SBUs reporting to them.

The reader will note that the strategic planning process is bi-centralized, with corporate and lower levels of general managers sharing authority and responsibility for the strategic development of the firm.

The bi-centralized structure evolved after early efforts to centralize strategic planning at the corporate level repeatedly proved unsuccessful. Experience showed that the lack of success was due to two factors: the first was a planning overload at the corporate level. The second, and more important factor was resistance to change by lower level managers. The phenomenon of resistance to change is discussed in Chapter 12.

To summarize, portfolio optimization involves corporate management in four ways:

- as provider of strategic guidance,
- evaluator of competitive posture plans,
- optimizer of the portfolio, and

implementer of mergers, acquisitions, and divestments.

Corporate management uses portfolio optimization for two distinct reasons. First, is management preference:

- When the corporate management has an entrepreneurial vision of continuously building a bigger and better firm.
- When the management style of the key managers is to play a strong directive role in the strategic evolution of the firm.

The second reason for the use of portfolio optimization are as follows:

- When the firm's near and long term growth/profitability prospects are unbalanced.
- When the future prospects will be discontinuous from the past.
- When the combined prospects offered by the firm's present portfolio are unsatisfactory.

As the reader recognizes, these conditions are encountered at Turbulence Levels 4 and 5.

Figure 9.2 shows a list of the components of the *portfolio posture*, which is the output of *portfolio optimization*. Each component is briefly discussed, starting with the strategic vision.

Figure 9.2
COMPONENTS OF THE PORTFOLIO POSTURE

ENVIRONMENT

SBA   SBA   SBA   SBA

Competitive   Competitive   Competitive   Competitive
Posture 1   Posture 2   Posture 3   Posture 4

PORTFOLIO POSTURE:
- Organization's Mission/Vision of the Future
- Corporate Goals and Objectives
- Portfolio Strategy – Diversification/Divestment Strategy
- Corporation's General Management Capability
- Corporate Strategic Budget
- Organization's Strategy Synergy

© H.I. Ansoff 1992

9.3 Management Vision

Management vision, alternatively called *strategic vision* or *management creed*, describes the shape of the firm that the influential managers of the firm propose to develop.

In some firms, the charismatic leader of the firm enunciates the vision. An example is Mr. Jack Welch of GE, who announced that he wanted General Electric to be a company that is technology-based doing business in the growth areas of the economy.

In other firms, such as the Johnson and Johnson Corp. (which calls its vision the firm's Creed), many levels of management are involved in periodic discussions of the vision. These discussions revise the vision to reflect changing aspirations of the influential stakeholders of the firm and the changing realities of the firm's external environment.

9.4 Corporate Goals and Objectives

It will be recalled that Long Range Planning sets goals (the levels of performance) for objectives (characteristics of performance, such as growth and profitability) which are assumed to be permanent.

Portfolio Optimization continually challenges the historical objectives. A master list from which firms choose their objectives is shown in Figure 9.3. The list shows four categories of objectives: performance, risk, synergy, and social objectives.

In environments whose changeability is at Level 4, the future prospects are expected to be discontinuous from the past, and growth no longer guarantees profitability. In such environments, it becomes necessary to replace the historical single growth objective with the four sub-objectives shown on the right of the figure.

In environments in which predictability is at level 4 and above, it becomes necessary to add two risk objectives: *invulnerability objective*, which protects the firm from strategic surprises, and *flexibility objective*, which positions the firm in future growth SBAs.

The synergy objective aims at assuring similarities among the management and functional capabilities that are required for successful management in the firm's SBAs. This objective may be pursued by a firm for one (or both) of two reasons:

1. To enable corporate management to play a strong directive role in the strategic development of the firm.

2. To enhance the overall performance of the firm through sharing common skills, technologies, and facilities among the SBAs of the firm.

Finally, in most industrialized countries, firms must increasingly include social objectives which seek to satisfy aspirations of the firm's employees and contribute to the needs of society. These actions maybe voluntary, forced by legislation, or under societal pressure.

9.5 Tradeoffs Among Goals

Contrary to Figure 9.3, historically successful firms typically specify only two performance goals, one for growth and another for profitability. This was completely adequate in environments up to Level 3 Turbulence.

Beyond Level 3, it becomes necessary to differentiate between near and long term goals in the manner shown in Figure 9.3: short term goals for the firm's competitive activity, and long-term goals for the strategic activity.

Figure 9.3

CORPORATE OBJECTIVES AND GOALS

PERFORMANCE: **NEAR TERM GROWTH**
LONG TERM GROWTH
NEAR TERM PROFITABILITY
LONG TERM PROFITABILITY

RISK: **INVULNERABILITY**
FLEXIBILITY

SYNERGY: **MANAGEMENT**
FUNCTIONAL

SOCIAL: **EMPLOYEES**
SOCIETAL

© H.I. Ansoff 1992

In practice however, investment in both long and short-term goals is made in the near term, because of the lead times in strategic development. Not only must the strategic investment be made in the near term, but also according to the prevalent accounting convention, this investment must be written off against the current profits of the firm, thus reducing near-term profitability.

As a result, long and short-term goals come into conflict with each other: overachievement in the short-term destroys the long-term performance and vice versa.

Similar conflicts occur among other goals. For instance, the risk goals are in conflict with the performance goals because they increase the number of the firm's SBAs and reduce the economies of scale which the firm could obtain by limiting its portfolio to a small number of SBAs.

The risk goals, by seeking to position the firm in dissimilar SBAs, also come into conflict with the synergy goals, which call for similarities among the SBAs.

Finally, the social goals can be in conflict with the performance goals because they divert cash flow from business activities into social pursuits.

As a result of the goal conflicts, the process of optimizing the SBA portfolio becomes very complex. The process is made even more complex and difficult by the fact that the respective goals are not comparable. For example, how does one compare a risk goal requiring that more than 20% should be vulnerable to a strategic surprise, to the profitability goal, which seeks a steady 20% ROI?

The answer to this question is that no quantitative techniques are available for making direct comparison of goals, and that judgmental comparison and adjustment of goals must be made by experienced corporate managers.

While this answer may be unsatisfactory to a quantitatively oriented reader, the fact of the matter is that experienced managers make such qualitative tradeoffs daily in a wide variety of decisions. Therefore, the process of portfolio optimization must be designed to involve corporate managers in the process. Such a design will be discussed after a few brief remarks about the concept of strategy.

9.6 Portfolio Strategy

The objectives and goals specify the results which the firm seeks to achieve. The Portfolio Strategy establishes the strategic development logic by which the objectives/goals will be achieved.

Figure 9.2 shows components of the portfolio posture strategy. The meaning of the components is self-explanatory with the possible exception of synergy.

Strategic synergy is the strategy component for meeting the firm's synergy objective. Management Synergy sub-strategy specifies the types of complementary capabilities that will be developed between corporate and SBU managements and SBA needs. Functional capabilities are specific capabilities that will be shared by the SBUs.

It is important to point out that functional synergy is not a natural characteristic of the firm, since each SBU manager naturally seeks to have a complete range of capabilities under his/her control. Therefore, unless continuously managed and reinforced from the corporate level, functional synergy is not likely to occur. On the other hand, management synergy is a welcomed characteristic and is attractive to corporate management, because it enhances its understanding of the SBU's problems and thus enhances the opportunity to play a constructive and directive role in corporate development. The recent wave of strategic rationalizations, mentioned earlier, in which firms reduce their portfolio and make the remaining SBAs more coherent and manageable by the corporate office, gives strong evidence of growing recognition of the importance of management synergy.

9.7   Portfolio Optimization Strategy

In view of the complexity of the portfolio optimization process, there is no opportunity to discuss it in detail in this volume. Instead, the principle steps in the process are presented. The process involves managers and their analytic staff in a joint step-by-step decision-making process which eventually results in the choice of the optimal portfolio.

The portfolio optimization strategy process works as follows:

1. The present portfolio strategy is diagnosed by analyzing the totality of the competitive posture plans for the SBAs.
2. The present portfolio is compared to the strategic vision. Either the strategy or the vision is modified until the strategy is acceptable.
3. A strategic budget is prepared for the acceptable strategy.
4. The strategic budget is compared to the resources that will be available to the firm for strategic investment. An infeasible strategy is sent back to the "drawing board".
5. Performance forecasts are made for the feasible strategy. This requires input of the profitability, growth, vulnerability prospects, which had previously been developed in the SBA plans.
6. The forecasts are compared to the goals set by the corporate management. If the portfolio does not meet the goals, either the goals are scaled down, or the strategy is sent back to the "drawing board". The strategy that finally meets the goals is chosen as the optimal strategy.
7. The final step is to design the future corporate capability that will be needed to support the chosen strategy.

This completes the discussion of the positioning strategic response, which sets out the path of the firm's strategic development into the future. As it has been demonstrated, the response is in two parts: planning the competitive posture for each SBA of the firm, and integrating the competitive postures into the overall strategic posture. The overall logic of the process is summarized in Figure 9.4, which the reader of the preceding pages can use to check his/her understanding of the preceding discussion.

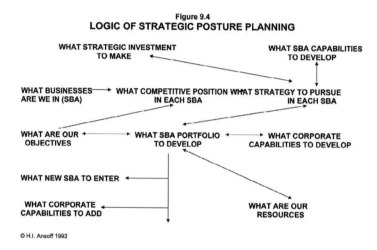

Figure 9.4
LOGIC OF STRATEGIC POSTURE PLANNING

© H.I. Ansoff 1992

The discussion continues with the strategic responses that become necessary when the predictability of the environment moves to Level 4.

CHAPTER 10
REAL TIME STRATEGIC RESPONSES

To deal with fast moving discontinuities when there are high levels of turbulence, firms have developed real time response systems: strategic issue management, weak signals response, and strategic surprise management.

In Chapter 8 two strategic responses were introduced: positioning response and *real time response.* The positioning response was discussed for both business and corporate levels in Chapters 8 and 9. Chapter 10 deals with *real time response.*

The anticipatory positioning systems, such as strategic planning and strategic posture planning, are increasingly inadequate for dealing with partially predictable Turbulence Levels of 4 and 5. In these high levels of turbulence discontinuities surface and impact on the firm too rapidly to be dealt with only by the positioning systems introduced earlier.

To deal with such fast moving discontinuities, firms have developed "real time" response systems. Three such systems will be examined:

1. Strategic Issue Management
2. Weak Signals and Graduated Responses
3. Strategic Surprise Management

10.1 Strategic Issue Management

The first real time response system, called strategic issue management, is illustrated in Figure 10.1. The system is simple to install and manage, and does not interfere with the existing structure and systems.

The issue management system works as follows:

1. Continuous surveillance is instituted over potential future external business - technological - economic - political- social - competitive discontinuities, which are likely to have a

significant impact on the firm. In large and geographically dispersed firms, the internal environment may also be surveyed for potential discontinuities in organizational effectiveness.

2. As each discontinuity is perceived, its impact on the firm and urgency of an immediate response are estimated. High impact discontinuities are labeled strategic issues.

3. As Figure 10.1 shows, each discontinuity is assigned to one of four categories:
   - High impact and highly urgent issues are earmarked for immediate response.
   - High impact issues of moderate urgency are earmarked for response during the next annual planning cycle.
   - High impact issues of low urgency are earmarked for continued surveillance.
   - Discontinuities whose impact is expected to be low are placed in a "dead file" and pursued no further.

4. The highly urgent issues are assigned for immediate resolution, either to an organizational unit, or to a special task force. The manager of the task force group is given the necessary resources and authority to demand assistance from any relevant part of the firm.

5. The moderately urgent issues are accumulated until the start of the next annual planning cycle and are made a part of the strategic guidelines. (See Chapter 9)

6. The low urgency issues are assigned for continual monitoring and evaluation to an individual or an organizational unit. If a periodic evaluation shows that the issue has become urgent, it is moved into category (1) or (2) above. If an evaluation shows that the impact will not be high, as originally estimated, the issue is placed in the "dead file".

Figure 10.1

STRATEGIC ISSUE MANAGEMENT

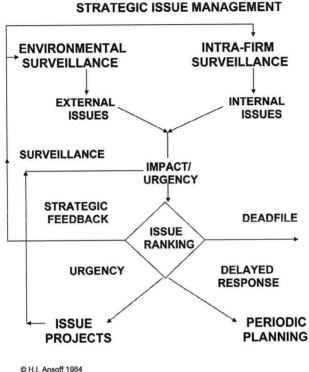

© H.I. Ansoff 1984

As the preceding discussion indicates, effective issue management requires assignment of responsibility for the several stages in the issue management process:

1. Responsibility for monitoring is typically assigned to a corporate forecasting unit.
2. Issue evaluation and classification is assigned to a planning unit.

A group of corporate (or group) general managers must assume authority and responsibility for assigning authority, responsibility, and resources to the units and task forces charged with urgent response to the issues.

This is an illustration of the stages and accountability typically found in large organizations. However, the very same stages need to be followed in small organizations with managers filling in the essential roles.

As the reader will readily perceive, issue management is very "light weight", flexible and simple, when compared to the annual planning cycle. But, to succeed, it must have time, attention and the commitment of a powerful group of general managers.

10.2 Weak Signals and Graduated Responses

Issues identified through environmental surveillance will differ in the amount of information they contain. Some issues will be sufficiently visible and concrete to permit the firm to develop specific and timely responses. These are called strong signal issues.

Other issues will be weak signals, imprecise early indications about impending impactful events. For example, it is clear today that, during the next few years, Asia and the Middle-East will be the source of important political upheavals, but it is not possible to predict with confidence where and when they will occur, nor what specific shape they will take.

Such weak signals mature over time and become strong issues. When the Turbulence Level is around 3 to 4, the firm can afford to wait until such issues become strong and unambiguous before initiating a response. But at Levels 4 to 5, when the speed of change is fast, if the firm waits until the signals become strong, the issue will have impacted on the firm before it has completed its response. Therefore, at high Turbulence Levels, it becomes necessary to start the firm's response while the environmental signals are still weak, and there is not enough information to formulate a clear and unambiguous response.

Identification and evolution procedures are very similar in weak and strong signal issue management systems. The difference between them lies in the responses to the signals. In the strong signal systems, it is possible to select a definitive response to the incoming signal. In weak signal systems there is not enough information for a definitive response to the threats or opportunities implied by the incoming signal. Therefore, the response has to be preparatory.

Figure 10.2 shows the preparatory responses. The top line of the figure describes the strength of the signal, which evolves over time.

Figure 10.2

POSSIBLE RESPONSES AT SIGNAL STRENGTH LEVELS

SIGNAL STRENGTH LEVEL / RESPONSE	1 SENSE OF TURBULENCE	2 SOURCE OF TURBULENCE	3 DISCONTINUOUS EVENT	4 RESPONSE IDENTIFIED	5 OUTCOME PREDICTABLE	6 IMPACT FELT
STRATEGIC	ENHANCE SURVEILLANCE	DIVERSIFY RISK	CREATE RESPONSE	LAUNCH HIGH RISK RESPONSE	LAUNCH LOW RISK RESPONSE	LAUNCH CATCH UP RESPONSE
CAPABILITY	AUDIT FLEXIBILITY	INCREASE FLEXIBILITY	ACQUIRE BASIC TECHNOLOGY	BUILD MINIMAL CAPABILITY	BUILD FULL SCALE CAPABILITY	CRASH BUILDUP OF CAPABILITY

© H.I. Ansoff 1992

The weakest signal on Level I is a sense of turbulence: there is enough information in the incoming weak signal to convince management that the future is going to be turbulent and very likely to produce novel threats and/or opportunities.

As time passes, the sense of turbulence is replaced by identification of the source from which the threats/opportunities will come. For example, today, there is a consensus among experts that a process called atomic fusion, which is now being studied in laboratories around the world, will eventually provide a source of non-polluting atomic energy (level 3).

In the atomic fusion example, levels 4, 5 and 6 will be arrived at as information about commercial products based on the atomic fusion process is accumulated, and commercial products are developed and established in the market place (level 6).

The lower two lines of Figure 10.2 show strategy and capability changes that can be made in firms, as the signal strength increases.

10.3 Strategic Surprise Management

Just as in a radar-surveillance system, in spite of the best efforts, some issues will slip by the environmental surveyors and become *strategic surprises*. This means four things:

1. The issue arrives suddenly, *unanticipated*.
2. It poses *novel* problems in which the firm has little prior experience.
3. Failure to respond implies either a *major financial reversal or loss* of a major opportunity.
4. The response is *urgent* and cannot be handled promptly enough by the existing systems and procedures.

The combination of the four factors creates major problems. The previous strategies and plans do not apply, the challenge is unfamiliar, and there is a flood of new information to process and to analyze. Thus, the firm is in danger of information overload. The suddenness and the prospects of a major loss, usually widely perceived throughout the organization, create a danger of widespread panic.

Perhaps most importantly, decentralized initiatives, which expedite response in competitive management, become ineffective and even potentially dangerous in a strategic surprise. Lacking a coherent strategy of response, local managers are likely to move the firm in "all directions at the same time" and create havoc. Finally, preoccupation with morale and the surprise are likely to divert attention from the continuing operations of producing, selling, and' distributing the organization's products and services.

If the firm expects its environmental turbulence to be around level five, it needs to invest in yet another system: a strategic surprise system. The characteristics of such a system are illustrated in Figure 10.3.

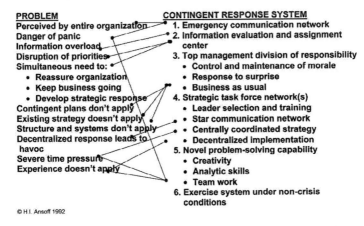

Figure 10.3
EMERGENCY RESPONSE TO STRATEGIC SURPRISE

PROBLEM
Perceived by entire organization
Danger of panic
Information overload
Disruption of priorities
Simultaneous need to:
• Reassure organization
• Keep business going
• Develop strategic response
Contingent plans don't apply
Existing strategy doesn't apply
Structure and systems don't apply
Decentralized response leads to havoc
Severe time pressure
Experience doesn't apply

CONTINGENT RESPONSE SYSTEM
1. Emergency communication network
2. Information evaluation and assignment center
3. Top management division of responsibility
   • Control and maintenance of morale
   • Response to surprise
   • Business as usual
4. Strategic task force network(s)
   • Leader selection and training
   • Star communication network
   • Centrally coordinated strategy
   • Decentralized implementation
5. Novel problem-solving capability
   • Creativity
   • Analytic skills
   • Team work
6. Exercise system under non-crisis conditions

© H.I. Ansoff 1992

The characteristics illustrated in Figure 10.3 are as follows:

1. When strategic surprise arrives, an emergency communication network goes into effect. The network crosses normal organizational boundaries, filters the information and rapidly communicates it to the entire organization.

2. For the duration of the emergency, the responsibilities of top management are repartitioned:

   • One group devotes its attention to the control and maintenance of organizational morale.

   • Another group assures continuance of "business as usual" with a minimum of disruptions.

   • A third group takes charge of response to the surprise.

3. For dealing with the surprises, a strategic task force network is activated.

   • Leaders and task force members cross normal organizational lines and constitute strategic action (not just planning) units.

   • The communication is of the "star shape" directly between the task forces and the central top management group.

   • The top management group formulates the overall strategy, assigns implementation responsibilities and coordinates the implementation.

- The decentralized task forces formulate and implement strategies within their areas of responsibility.
4. The task force and communication networks are redesigned and trained.
   - Several networks may be redesigned: one to deal with surprises in the market place, another with technological surprises, a third to deal with political surprises, etc.
   - The task forces are trained to respond promptly to novel problems. Their response combines creativity with analytical techniques.
5. The networks are exercised under non-crisis conditions in addressing real strategic issues, as if they were surprises.

The cross-connecting lines in Figure 10.3 show how the respective characteristics of the surprise management system respond to the problems and challenges posed by a strategic surprise.

10.4 Choosing Strategic Responses for a Firm

The positioning response is determined by the changeability of the environment and the real time response by its predictability.

At a given point in time, the turbulence levels which measure changeability and predictability may be different. For example, an SBA may be facing the prospect of a major and fully predictable discontinuity such as saturation of market demands; and in another SBA growth prospects may be extrapolable from the past, but weak signals indicate that the extrapolated trend may be upset by surpriseful events, such as invasion of the industry by an alternative technology that serves the same need.

Figures 10.4 and 10.5 summarize the organization's positioning responses and tools used in each level of turbulence,

Figure 10.4

CHOOSING POSITIONING RESPONSE

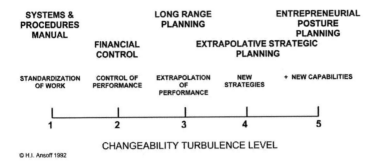

© H.I. Ansoff 1992

The lower part of Figure 10.4 shows the success behaviors needed by an organization at each of the Turbulence levels. Figure 10.5 illustrates the corresponding responses at each Turbulence Level.

This completes the discussion of choice of responses. In the next we turn our attention to the implementation process of the chosen responses.

Figure 10.5

CHOOSING REAL TIME RESPONSE

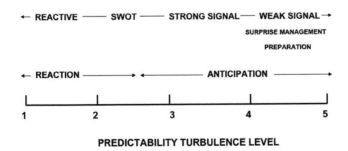

© H.I. Ansoff 1992

CHAPTER 11
STRATEGIC POSTURE IMPLEMENTATION

The process that converts strategic plans into reality is called the strategy implementation process. However, a more accurate name is strategic posture implementation. There are two major types of resistance to change: systemic and behavioral.

11.1   Resistance to Change

In the preceding pages there was a review of the decision making process involved in the development of plans for the firm's future strategic posture: the competitive and portfolio strategies, the organizational capability, and the strategic investment.

The next concern of general management is to transform the plans into reality. Several actions are required: new SBAs entered, obsolete SBAs divested, new technologies acquired new product/service lines developed, new marketing strategies put in place, new capabilities ready to support the new strategic activities. The process that converts strategic plans into reality is called the *strategy implementation* process. However, a more accurate name is strategic posture implementation.

When strategic planning was first invented in the 1960's, the firm's ability to implement the new strategic plans was implicitly taken for granted. The firms that invented strategic planning had been successful implementers of competitive plans for many years, and it was assumed that strategic implementation was not different from competitive implementation.

Experience quickly showed that this assumption was inaccurate. At best, strategic changes were much slower than anticipated, resulting in major time slippages and unanticipated costs. At worst, strategic plans never got to the market place, resulting in a common phenomenon, which was named *paralysis by analysis.*

If, after several fruitless planning cycles, paralysis by analysis persisted, the strategic planning gradually ground to a halt, thus producing a phenomenon that was named *death in the drawer* (of the planner's desk).

Early diagnosis ascribed the cause of these phenomena to resistance to *planning,* or *resistance to change,* and the explanation was that the plan failures were due to a lack of understanding by managers of the benefits to firm which were to be brought about by the new strategic posture.

The recommended remedy was to have the Chief Executive Officer communicate to the organization his/her belief and commitment to strategic planning and explain its benefits.

Experience showed that this remedy produced, at best, temporary results. At the present time there is widespread concern among general managers with strategic implementation. Fortunately, experience and research have produced a much better understanding of what causes resistance to change and the ways to minimize and manage resistance. A summary of the current thought in this area is given in the following pages.

11.2 Conflict of Strategic and Operating Work

Strategic planning and implementation impose a large workload, both on management and on the rest of the firm. This workload typically comes on top of a demanding and time consuming workload of daily competitive behaviour. If a firm is well run, there are no "idle hands" waiting to receive the strategic workload. Thus, a conflict for capacity is inevitable: if the new strategic work is to be done, the competitive work must yield some of the time and resources that are fully employed in the competitive work.

Repeated experience has shown that when an organization is confronted with the capacity conflict, the daily preoccupation and pressures of competitive work win over the long term concerns about future profitability. Hence, a common phrase which is familiar to all experienced managers: "tomorrow we will get organized and plan, but today we have real work to do".

Several solutions are available for minimizing the capacity conflict:

1.Increase total organizational capacity to accommodate both types of work. Many years ago Peter Drucker proposed a sure-fire solution for assuring that strategic work will receive proper attention. This solution was to introduce a *dual budgeting system* into the firm, which separated the total budget into a competitive budget and a strategic *budget*. As every manager knows the best way to create capacity is to allocate a budget.

2. Increased capacity will make possible, but will not guarantee that strategic work will receive its share of attention. This is because the new capacity will be in danger of being subverted by the competitive work. In fact, there is a Gresham's Law of Planning, formulated by Nobel Prize winner Herbert Simon, which states that competitive work drives out strategic work. Therefore, strategic work must be protected from the competitive work by creating special units within the firm that are dedicated to the strategic work.

This approach is now receiving a great deal of attention in business practice. For example, the General Electric Company set up separate corporate entities within the firm with their own respective boards of directors, management and facilities, dedicated to strategic/entrepreneurial activities.

LockheedMartin Corporation has used another similar solution successfully for many years. They set up a physically separated advanced development group, which reports directly to the Chief Executive Officer of the organization.

3. A third and complementary approach to resolving the capacity conflict is to offer rewards for strategic work. Curiously enough, many firms that are habitual users of strategic planning still use reward and incentive systems that reward only competitive work. The design of strategic reward and incentive systems is another area that is currently receiving increased attention in many organizations.

11.3 Lack of Strategic Competence

As the previous discussion has demonstrated, successful strategic management requires a profile of management competence which is very different from competitive management. The reader can quickly realize the difference by referring and comparing the management profile at Level 4, which is needed for strategic work, to profiles for Levels 2 and 3 which optimize a firm's competitive success.

As in the case of capacity conflict, introduction of strategic planning has typically been undertaken without attention being paid to the need to change the firm's competence profile. When this is done, another phenomenon surfaces which is called **GIGO** ("garbage in-garbage out"): the quality of planning is poor and the outputs are not implementable.

The solution to the incompetence problem is to develop the necessary and appropriate competence profile, as described in Chapter 8. It should be emphasized that the new competence is not a replacement but an addition to the existing competence. Therefore, competence development must be accompanied by resolving the capacity conflict described above.

11.4 Types of Resistance to Change

There are two major types of resistance to change: *systemic* and *behavioral.* Systemic resistance is the one stemming from the organization itself as a system and behavioral comes from the individual or groups within the organization.

Systemic Resistance:

Lack of capacity and competence produces what is called systematic resistance to discontinuous change. It causes delays, overruns, and blockages because the plans are of low quality and are not implementable. Systematic resistance is proportional to the incapacity, incompetence and conflict between the strategic and operating work. An illustration of the systemic resistance presented in Figure 11. 1

Figure 11.1

SYSTEMIC RESISTANCE IS PROPORTIONAL TO:

INCAPACITY

> **SHORTAGE OF BUDGETS**
> **SHORTAGE OF MANAGERS**
> **SHORTAGE OF FUNCTIONAL CAPACITY**

INCOMPETENCE

> **LACK OF STRATEGIC SKILLS (TURBULENCE)**
> **LACK OF STRATEGIC INFORMATION**
> **INAPPLICABILITY OF SYSTEMS/STRUCTURE**

CONFLICT OF STRATEGIC AND OPERATING WORK

> **GRESHAM'S LAW OF PLANNING**

© H.I. Ansoff, 1992

Behavioral Resistance:

A major source of behavioral resistance is the strategic myopia exhibited by the key decision makers in the firm. Experience has shown repeatedly that when top managers are presented with forecasts predicting a future world that is discontinuous from the past, the managers typically reject such forecasts as "unrealistic" and "impractical". This phenomenon of rejection of unfamiliar information is prevalent enough to have acquired the name of strategic myopia.

The cause of myopia is now well understood. Managers usually learn by trial and error. During their careers, they are continually called upon to evaluate environmental challenges and to act upon them. Evaluations and actions that succeed progressively build in the manager's mind a model of what is relevant to the firm, what is irrelevant, and what are the success factors in the environment. When a new signal is received from the environment, the manager (consciously or subconsciously) tests it for relevance to his/her mental model. If the signal is relevant, the manager accepts it and acts upon it. If the signal is not relevant the manager rejects it.

In the face of a discontinuity from past experience, the most myopic manager is likely to be one who has been very successful in the past.

Strategic Myopia is the most important element of behavioral resistance to change because only general management has the power to trigger change of a magnitude that will cause a radical departure from the historical course of the organization.

In recent years several methods have been developed and used which can help managers avoid myopia. Although different in detail, all of the methods involve helping managers to confront a discontinuous future through guided group problem solving.

Once myopia is overcome, general management has to turn attention to organizational resistance to change, which originates with individuals and groups in the rest of the organization.

Organizational resistance occurs when a discontinuous change evokes one or more of the following responses from the individuals and groups within the organization:

- sense of personal insecurity
- fear of being found incompetent in performing strategic work
- perception that the change is leading the firm astray by violating its historical success model
- perception that the new behaviour demanded by the change violates organizational norms and values
- recognition that no rewards are offered for the new behavior
- fear by groups and individuals of loss of power and influence as a result of the change
- fear of loss of status and prestige
- fear of loss or rewards which were offered for the historical behaviour

A perusal of the above list shows that in this case "to name the problem is to solve it". People can be reassured, they can be trained, appropriate rewards can be offered, people can be persuaded, that the historical success model must be changed if the firm is to remain successful. Therefore, behavioral resistance can be reduced substantially by addressing the fears and concerns of affected groups and individuals.

However, some of the concerns cannot be eliminated: some individuals and groups *will* lose power, some *will* lose prestige, some *will* lose rewards. Therefore, there is a residual behavioral resistance, largely due to the challenge to the historical power structure, which cannot be eliminated by explanation, education, training, and persuasion. This part of behavioral resistance must be overcome by application of power by general management.

11.5 Managing Resistance - A Summary

To summarize the preceding discussion, the phenomenon that has been called resistance to change originates from two sources:

1. *Systemic resistance is* caused by:
- capacity conflict between strategic and competitive work
- incompetence of the management organization in strategic planning and implementation.

2.*Behavioral resistance.* There are two behavioral sources:
- *Strategic myopia* of the key general managers, which is caused by the failure to anticipate and recognize the need for a discontinuous change.
- *Behavioral resistance* by the rest of the organization, which is caused by misunderstanding of the need and consequences of the change, threats to security of individuals and groups, and threats to the power structure posed by change.

Systemic resistance is a negative inertia phenomenon that can be eliminated by:
- building and protecting the capacity needed for strategic work
- developing a capability profile needed for effective planning and executing the change.

Myopia is a psychological phenomenon that can be converted into acceptance and support of the change:

- either by replacing managers who are myopic,
- or by helping these managers confront the future reality which makes the change imperative

Behavioral resistance is a cultural and political phenomenon. Cultural resistance can be eliminated and even converted into active support of change by:

- eliminating misperceptions of need and consequences of change,
- training and reassuring groups and individuals who fear the change, and
- transforming the organizational culture.

Much of the political resistance can be reduced by:

- reassuring groups and individuals who are not going to lose their power and status
- converting groups and individuals, who stand to gain power and influence from the change, into active supporters of the change.

However, in most discontinuous changes there are groups and individuals who will stand to lose power and influence. Their resistance can be dealt with by:

- either removing the individuals from their positions of power, or
- applying counter power to overcome the residual political resistance.

11.6 Dynamics of Managing Resistance

The strength of resistance that will be encountered is determined by two factors:

1. Resistance is proportional to the gap between the present capability profile and the profile needed to give enthusiastic and effective support to the change. This gap can be determined by conducting a strategic diagnosis.
2. The second determinant is the time period over which the

change spread. The resistance, which is encountered at a point in time during the change process, is inversely proportional to the time planned to complete the change. In other words, the longer the time, the less the resistance.

The two resistance factors, are summarized in the *resistance management equation* shown on the left side of Figure 11.2, where the symbol means "proportional".

Figure 11.2

RESISTANCE MANAGEMENT EQUATION

POTENTIAL RESISTANCE IS PROPORTIONAL TO THE GAP BETWEEN THE PRESENT PROFILE AND THE CHANGE SUPPORTING CAPABILITY PROFILE

BEHAVIORAL RESISTANCE CAN BE SUBSTANTIALLY REDUCED IN ADVANCE OF THE CHANGE

EXCEPT IN A CRISIS, RESIDUAL RESISTANCE REQUIRES APPLICATION OF POWER

THE POWER REQUIRED IS PROPORTIONAL TO THE RESISTANCE

$$P \propto R$$

$$R \propto \frac{\text{Capability}}{\text{Duration of Change}} = \frac{1}{t}$$

CONFLICT BETWEEN EXTERNAL AND INTERNAL "CLOCKS"

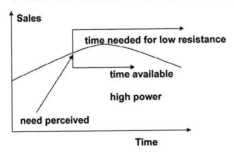

© H.I. Ansoff 1992

The right side of the figure shows the problem that confronts management in designing a discontinuous change. The sales curve in the figure will result if the firm fails to make timely discontinuous change in time to avert competitive threat in the market place.

At the point labeled "need perceived", the firm's management decides to design and launch a response which will avert the threat.

If management chooses to stretch the change over a time sufficient to guarantee low resistance, the effort will fail and sales would have declined precipitously long before the change process is completed.

The alternative is to choose a duration that will assure that the change will be completed in time to prevent the decline of sales. But this will require a coercive application of power, which will make the process costly, inefficient, and turbulent.

Thus, the problem confronted by general management can be stated as follows: The duration of the change process must be planned not to exceed the deadline determined by the imperatives of the environment, and the necessary power must be marshaled and applied to assure a timely completion of the change.

11.7   Strategies for Change Management- The Accordion Method

This leads us to the strategies for change management. There are a number of strategies for change, each applicable under specific circumstances. These strategies are illustrated in Figure 11.3.

Figure 11.3

STRATEGIES FOR CHANGE MANAGEMENT

STRATEGY	APPLICABILITY	ADVANTAGES	SHORTCOMINGS
CHARISMATIC VISION	High urgency	Speed Low resistance	Charismatic leadership is rare.
COERCIVE	High urgency	Speed	High resistance
CRISIS	Survival threat	Speed Low resistance	Extreme time pressure Failure risk
ORGANIC ADAPTATION	Low urgency	Low resistance	Slow
MANAGED RESISTANCE	Medium urgency	Timely change Minimum resistance	Complexity Must be planned and managed

© H.I. Ansoff 1992

The figure illustrates the circumstances under which each change management strategy is applicable, as well as the potential shortcomings of each. There are 'champions' for each of the methods. The various methods are readily self-explanatory except the last one, managed resistance.

Managed resistance is used when the installation timing of the implementation is known. It is used when there is medium level of urgency. Its advantage is that the installation speed can be altered based on competitor's responses, environmental changes and the readiness level of the organization.

The managed resistance change strategy method looks like an accordion, where each panel is a separate project/module building and affecting the final process. Thus, it can be called accordion strategic transformation. This process is illustrated in Figure 11.4.

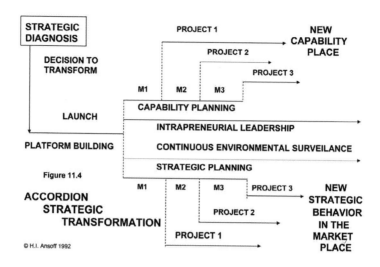

Figure 11.4

ACCORDION
STRATEGIC
TRANSFORMATION

© H.I. Ansoff 1992

The launching platform is depicted on the left and the final realization on the right. Both capability and strategy need to be installed to have the change process completed.

Each module consists of two parts translated into capability and strategy projects. Capability focuses on skill development resistance reduction, and strategy focuses on direction, plans and strategic positioning. The capability project takes place first because of the need to modify the behavior/skills first in order to help change the attitude to the realization of the 'new environment'. This new perspective helps execute the strategy project with the 'new' mindset.

Each module is clearly monitored by measurable results. During the installation of each module there is a constant review of the external environment to assess the speed of installation against the movable overall target time frame. (It is movable because of external environmental changes, making it essential to conduct continuous monitoring.)

If the installation falls behind schedule, the modules are accelerated. If the installation is ahead of the speed of response of the environment and its movable target date, then the modules could be decelerated. The latter response would produce less overall resistance.

The uniqueness of this process is that each module can be modified based on inputs from the previous modules and new information from the organization's external environment. Thus, the contraction and expansion, as well as the continuous input of new information about the external environment, produces better and more up-to-date results.

Figure 11.5 includes a list of items needed for the application of the Accordion method.

Figure 11.5
CHECK LIST FOR MANAGING ACCORDION TRANSFORMATION

CHOICE OF STRATEGY
1. Perform Strategic Diagnosis
2. Assess Urgency
3. Select Change Strategy

BUILDING LAUNCHING PLATFORM
1. Prepare Support/Resistance Map
2. Muster Support
3. Design Change Process:
   - Use accordion design to assure timely completion
   - Capability increments should precede strategy instruments
   - Appoint transformation manager(s)
   - Organize planning teams
   - Appoint resistance monitoring team
   - Select planning team

LAUNCH THE TRANSFORMATION
1. Communicate vision, need for change, expected results
2. Launch implementation projects after each module
3. Include planners in the implementation teams
4. Exercise controls
   - Strategy
   - Implementation
   - Resistance, use power only when necessary

© H.I. Ansoff 1992

It also includes a list of areas that need to be addressed and resolved before and during the application of the accordion method. There are three areas:

1. Strategy Choices
2. Building the Launching Platform, and
3. Launching the Transformation

11.8   The Intrapreneur

The person most suited for managing a transformation is an intrapreneur. The intrapreneur is a unique individual:

- a *visionary creator* of opportunities,
- a forceful *manager,* and
- an entrepreneur within an organization.

Figure 11.6 illustrates the behavior of an intrapreneur during transformations.

The figure depicts the behaviors of successful and unsuccessful managers during the three stages of the transformational process: sensing threats and opportunity, planning strategy, and implementing. These were the findings of an empirical study of 32 Swiss top SBU managers (Lombriser, Ansoff,1992).

The most successful intrapreneur triggers change early on, participates in the decision-making analysis and involves implementers (since they are the ones who know exactly what resources are needed and will be the ones to implement it). One of the unique contributions of an intrapreneur in the planning strategy stage is in the decision making process. It was found that a successful intrapreneur seeks consensus, but failing consensus he/she makes the decision. This is where the vision and forcefulness are the pivotal and distinct characteristics of an intrapreneur.

The intrapreneur remains involved in the implementation process in overseeing and revising the overall strategy.

This completes the exposition of the issues surrounding the strategy implementation process. The next Chapter deals with one of the areas of major concern to the corporate office, strategic management of technology.

Figure 11.6
BEHAVIOR OF GENERAL MANAGER
DURING STRATEGY TRANSFORMATION

OUTCOME	SENSING THREATS/ OPPORTUNITIES	PLANNING STRATEGY	IMPLEMENTING THE PLAN
MOST SUCCESSFUL	• Triggers change early on incomplete information	• Participates in decision analysis • Involves implementers • Makes decisions using explicit estimate of risk • Seeks consensus; failing consensus makes the decision	• Initiates implementation planning • Delegates detailed planning • Controls projects' performance • Revises strategy
LEAST SUCCESSFUL	• Triggers change after loss of performance	• Lets others perform decision analysis • Makes decisions using implicit risk judgments • Makes final decisions alone or • on absolute consensus by others	• Personally plans implementation or • Delegates all implementation planning to others

CHAPTER 12
STRATEGIC MANAGEMENT OF TECHNOLOGY

The creation, development and application of technology are major forces that make firms successful. In turbulent environments, technology strategy becomes an important component in the job of the general manager.

12.1 Technological Challenges to General Management

Technology was driving force in the 20th century and it promises to hold the same if not greater importance during the 21st. The creation, development and application of technology are major forces that make firms successful. The most successful and admired organizations are those that are in the forefront of technological innovations.

While general management is responsible for the firm's strategic direction, it frequently fails to manage the organization's technological innovation process in both low and high technology industries.

In low technology organizations the focus is primarily on utilizing and expanding technology innovation. In high technology organizations technology is one of the critical determining factors of a firm's future success. It is expected that high technology turbulence is going to increase and become one of the critical determining factors for an organization's future success. The emphasis in this chapter will be on the high technology turbulence levels.

Apple and IBM are examples of companies whose general managements were unsuccessful in managing their firms' technological innovations in the mid to late 80's. In both cases their general managers did not see the emerging technological as well as the business discontinuities and changes associated with them. Therefore, management became the enemy of their own successes. In both cases their general managers were asked to resign.

In the first part of this book we introduced a model of the modern firm consisting of the profit making and strategic development processes.

The management of a firm's technological innovation is part of its strategic development. Through technological innovation new technologies, product prototypes and the subsequent stream of new products are developed and explored. Selection of the wrong technologies and products as well as downstream mismanagement of a firm's profit making processes will lead to a decline of organizations' profitability.

12.2 Technological Variables Impact Strategy

There are external and internal variables that influence the organization's development and direction. The external variables are: *technological progress, technological turbulence,* and *product dynamics.* The internal ones are: *leadership role* and *power center.* These are described below:

Technological progress assesses the *competitive dynamics* of technology, technological product differentiation, use of technology as a competitive tool, as well as technological responses due to consumer pressures and governmental regulations. These dynamics influence the competitive and technological intensity of organization's technological environment. Technological progress can be:

- Incremental, where it is expected that extensions of existing technologies will prevail, i.e. the hygiene or industrial detergent industries, or
- Discontinuous, where inventions of new technologies are expected to emerge, i.e. digital technology in photography.

Technological turbulence determines the length of the *demand-technology life cycle*, the frequency introduction of new technologies to the market, and the number of competing technologies.

Product dynamics varies according to the frequency of new products introduced to the market, the length of the products' life cycles and technologies, incorporated in successive products.

The other two variables, leadership role and power center, are the internal ones and relate to an organization's desired position in the future.

Leadership role helps assess the organization's future *competitive position* in the market. The firm's role can be imitator, follower or leader. To make the decision on which role to play, general management needs to assess:

1. the competence level of the organization's technologists
2. the existence or not of technological obsolescence,
3. the firm's research leadership abilities,
4. the firm's leadership position in the market,
5. the firm's abilities to provide product/service support,
6. the processes that exist now, versus the ones that need to be in place to provide future product/service support.

Power center identifies the departments within the firm where the stimulus for new technology development originates. The different departments include production, marketing, R&D or general management.

The interpretation and assessment of the external and internal variables (See Figure 12.1) help general management chose the firm's technology strategy by:

1. forecasting the future technological turbulence,
3. diagnosing the firm's present technological aggressiveness,
4. determining the firm's future technology gap, and
5. designing actions and priorities for future technology development.

The process for determining the external and internal factors affecting the firm's technology strategy are discussed in Chapter 2.7 of Ansoff and McDonnell's book, *Implanting Strategic Management*.

Figure 12.1
TECHNOLOGY STRATEGY ANALYSIS

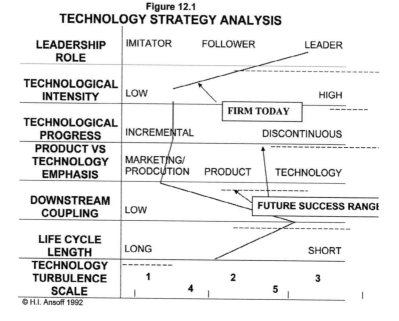

© H.I. Ansoff 1992

12.3 Technological Myopia

As has been discussed repeatedly in this book, in order to assure future success, an organization's strategic direction should be determined by anticipating the future needs of the environment. In today's turbulent environment, misinterpretation of the future environment will have impacts on the firm's future. To succeed in these environments, general managers need to have the mindset and skills to interpret the direction the environment is taking.

Addressing the problem of technological myopia is progressively becoming critical to the success of firms. Before general managers address problems relating to the firm's technologies, they need to realize that they themselves might be myopic. General managers' myopia needs to be treated first before addressing the existence, or not, of technological myopia.

Myopic general managers refuse to foresee new technological direction. Therefore, myopic general managers do not support technological developments in a direction that would be the most successful for their firm's future.

Figure 12.2 illustrates the events associated with technological myopia and its impact during technology substitution.

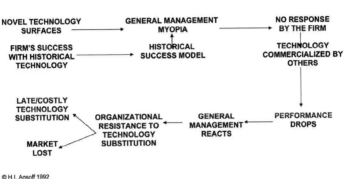

Figure 12.2
**TECHNOLOGICAL MYOPIA
DURING TECHNOLOGY SUBSTITUTION**

© H.I. Ansoff 1992

An example of this can be seen in the actions taken by Mr. Akers's, Lou Gerstner's predecessor at IBM, who took the company's reins in 1985. When Mr. Akers joined IBM, he found a firm that had "...developed the feeling that it could do no wrong. An absolute myopia developed about what was really happening out there with the customers" (Business Week Feb. 15, 1988). Mr. Akers did not interpret the demand, features and technological applications of personal computers correctly. He neither saw the shift of technology from hardware to software, nor the future potential of the personal computers. Personal computers were perceived as self-standing instruments, and were viewed as hardware pieces with limited capabilities. As a result, Mr. Akers did not see the value of expanding into the personal computer hardware industry where each unit is sold at a ridiculously low price in comparison to that of mainframes.

Lack of a correct interpretation of the trends in the computer industry and IBM's past successes on mainframe computers caused Mr. Akers to think that '...mainframe computers were here to stay forever'. IBM's general management made its decision to focus on mainframe computers based on the expertise and technical knowledge of individuals who were equally myopic, and whose backgrounds and experience were in mainframe technology.

IBM's lack of response encouraged competitors to introduce clones of the (PS/2) personal computers, thus, eroding IBM's market share.

In 1988, when Mr. Akers reacted belatedly and inconclusively, IBM's financial performance had been declining for two consecutive years. IBM reacted with a late and costly technology substitution.

In order to assess the direction of an organization's technology environments and reduce technological myopia, the collection of necessary information should come from a wide range of unbiased sources, from within as well as from outside the firm.

General managers need to seek advice especially from outside the firm in order to:

1. examine the existence of technological myopia of the firm's technologists, and

2. understand and get an unbiased view of the future technology developments in the firm's industry.

The analysis of the information from within as well as from outside the organization forces general managers to question their firm's technological competence in the industry.

In turbulent environments general managers are the ones assessing and interpreting the information on the firm's technology developments.

Assessment and interpretation of information on future technologies encompasses dealing with employees and outside experts, whose-knowledge and expertise is in a field where general managers might not have the desired background or knowledge. Therefore, general managers need to develop some knowledge in the technology field and most importantly to develop their skill in using experts and asking experts 'expert questions'. The development of these skills is discussed later in the chapter.

12.4 The Role of General Management in Technology Innovation

In managing an organization's technology innovation in turbulent environments, general managers should:

1. guide the firm's forecasting units,

2. direct the firm's technology innovation process,
3. assure the level of competence of the firm's technologists,
4. direct production and marketing for timely introduction of products/ services to the market, and
5. choose the firm's technology strategy.

In turbulent environments the use of cutting edge technology is a critical success factor. Therefore, general managers need to assure that the firm has up-to-date technology that will support the firm's business strategy.

Technological Turbulence

Figure 12.3 shows three possible levels of technological turbulence.

Figure 12.3
DEMAND-TECHNOLOGY-PRODUCT LIFE CYCLES

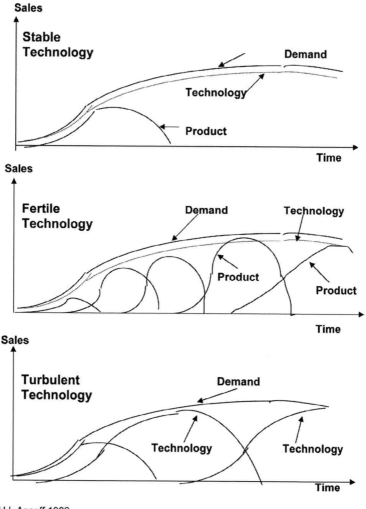

© H.I. Ansoff 1992

The upper graph demonstrates a stable, long-lived technology, which remains basically unchanged for the duration of the demand life cycle. This graph describes many of the first generation industries that were founded at the end of the nineteenth century and began to reach maturity in the 1950's.

The middle graph illustrates what we shall call fertile technologies. The basic technology is long-lived, but products proliferate, offering progressively better performance, and broadening the field of application. In fertile technologies, for example, in the data processing and pharmaceutical industries, product development becomes a critical factor in economic success. The newest and best performing product captures the market. This usually takes place by developing additional applications, uses or extensions of existing technologies, for example, the watch industry or the sheet glass industry.

The third graph in Figure 12.3 demonstrates a turbulent field of technology in which one or more basic technology substitutions take place within the life span of the demand life cycle. Success in a turbulent field of technology requires the invention of new technologies which replace the existing ones, for example, the office automation or the audio industry.

The effects of technology substitution are further reaching than that of product fertility. Technology substitution threatens obsolescence of the firm's entire investment in the preceding technology.

The role of general managers is to guide their firm's forecasting units in collecting and interpreting information on the firm's future environment. This information will indicate whether the firm will be operating in fertile, turbulent or both fertile and turbulent technological environments.

Based on the information general managers receive on the firm's future technology environments from outside as well as from within the firm, general managers decide on their firm's R&D direction.

Transition to a new technology is difficult within the firm, not only financially, but also culturally and politically. The new technology challenges the historical success model held by both technologists and general managers. It also threatens the position of power and influence within the firm.

The problem of transition to a new technology is further aggravated when the technology is both fertile and turbulent. When a new technology surfaces, the firm is already deeply involved in the competitive struggle of product proliferation. Its R&D program is committed to this struggle and can become an obstacle to the firm's transition to the new substituting technology. This is exactly what happened at Eastman Kodak when digital technology emerged as the next generation of technology in image processing.

General managers need to decide whether the firm will be operating in:

1. a fertile technological environment, thus requiring investment in extension of technologies to satisfy future needs, or
2. a turbulent technological environment, thus requiring investment in invention of technologies to satisfy future needs, or
3. both a fertile and turbulent technological environment, thus requiring separation of the firm's efforts between extension and invention of future technologies.

General managers do not always interpret future direction of technology correctly. An example is Remington typewriters. Remington's technological advantage was the 'feather touch' feature of its typewriter. This is what gave Remington a differentiating advantage in the marketplace. Under management's direction, Remington's R&D division focused on how to extend the existing technology by trying to make the 'feather touch' more 'feather touch'. IBM surpassed Remington by introducing a replacement technology, the electric typewriter and the new 'ball' design, which made IBM well known in the 1970's.

The same case scenario occurred later with IBM. IBM was still introducing new and upgraded models of the electric 'ball' technology typewriters, while IBM's competitors gained market advantage by introducing a completely different type of technology, the word processors and later the desk top computers. The products/ technologies replaced typewriters completely.

The challenge to management is to be realistic in assessing the consequences of the new technology. It is easy to rationalize that a new technology will revolutionize the products and produce a large-scale revival demand. This is not likely to occur, unless the advances are so revolutionary to make obsolete the products that already saturate the marketplace.

12.5 The Role of General Managers in Assuring the Level of Competence of Their Firm's Technologists

Technologists play a significant role in introducing new technologies and consequently products/services to the market. Their role is to focus on development of new technologies and products. They hold in their hands creative process of new technology development.

Technology is translated into new inventions, new applications and/ or products and services. New technologies are obtained through long term investment directly impacting the firm's short-term profitability.

It is necessary for general managers and their firm's technologists to communicate pertinent information to each other in order for general managers to determine the firm's future direction. Particularly in turbulent environments, general managers must become involved in the management of technology articulate the products and services general management desires. Furthermore, general managers need to assure themselves that the necessary technological expertise exists within the firm to develop the needed products/ services.

In high turbulent environments the problem of obsolescence of a firm's technologists could develop. When a new technology evolves it is likely that expertise of the existing technologists could become obsolete. It is necessary for general managers to assess whether their firm's technologists have the needed expertise for the new technology.

Obsolete technologists can become an obstacle to the firm's technological innovation. They are usually the ones who introduced a technology with a successful stream of products/services which is becoming obsolete. They do not see the next technological wave.

When there is technological obsolescence, general management separates the firm's technologists into three groups, based on their expertise. The first group consists of the technologists who are experts on the existing technology. Their focus is on extension, and support of existing technologies.

The second group consists of technologists who are experts in the existing technology, but are trainable in the new technology the firm wants to develop in the future. This group would focus on training in and the development of the new technology and would later be screened based on the individual's progress and development.

Technologists whose expertise lies in the next generation of technologies the firm wishes to develop in the future form the third group. Their instructions are to develop the new generation of technology and are given the appropriate resources. These technologists are separated as a group because they should not be 'contaminated' or 'stifled' by the technologists and mindsets committed to the previous technology.

A company that followed this approach successfully is Eastman Kodak. General management separated the technologists of image processing into two groups. The first was comprised of technologists of the silver halide technology, which Eastman Kodak pioneered and with what it dominates the U.S. and global markets. The focus of this group is on the proliferation of the halide technology.

The second group is focusing on the digital technology, its Great-ion, evolution and the generation of products that Eastman Kodak will be adopting in the near future.

Other companies that followed this approach successfully were Walt Disney, with the animation group, and Lockheed, with the Stealth project.

12.6 Gaps between General Managers and Technologists

In relating with each other, general managers and technologists have different views of reality and are typically confronted with several gaps in understanding each other. These gaps are the *semantic gap,* the *objectives/value gap,* and, the *information gap.*

These gaps are illustrated in Figure 12.4.

Figure 12.4
GAPS BETWEEN
GENERAL MANAGEMENT AND TECHNOLOGISTS

INFORMATION GAP
NEEDS:
GENERAL MANAGEMENT: TECHNOLOGICAL HORIZONS

TECHNOLOGISTS: **STRATEGIC GUIDANCE**

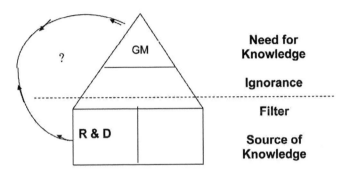

SEMANTIC GAP
*MENTALITY DIFFERENCES
*LANGUAGE DIFFERENCES
*IMPLICIT KNOWLEDGE: "Fingerspitzengefuhl"

OBJECTIVES/VALUE GAP
GENERAL MANAGEMENT: OPTIMIZE ROI
TECHNOLOGISTS: ***OPTIMIZE KNOWLEDGE**
                              *SOCIAL PROGRESS
                              *PRESTIGE
                              *THRILL OF DISCOVERY

© H.I. Ansoff 1984

The *semantic gap* arises from differences in language and perception of success factors between general managers and the firm's technologists.

While general managers focus on operations and technological advancements, technologists perceive technological advancements and breakthroughs as the critical success factors in their profession. Technologists typically perceive technological variables as the decisive parameters in advocating new investment.

The key is how general managers and technologists communicate their needs so that each one utilizes their implicit knowledge.

The *objectives/value gap* arises from the difference in what is perceived to be important.

General managers concentrate on the commercial impact of technology and are interested in providing support for technological advancements based on expected commercial impact.

The emphasis of technologists is more on the thrill of discovery, which is translated in the optimization of knowledge, research, social progress and the professional prestige associated with it. The firm's profitability can be more of a hindrance rather than a stimulus for technologists. Profitability usually stifles the development process, questioning the researchers' reasoning of further exploration in every step. While technologists see a technological innovation as enough of a reason to bring it to the market, general managers need to realize its profit potential.

The *information gap* arises from the knowledge and information that general managers and technologists need from each other. On one hand, general managers need to have knowledge of the technological prospects in order to decide on future technology development. Technologists, on the other hand, need to have strategic guidance to direct the technology efforts for research and exploration.

Knowledge on new technologies is often vague and difficult to quantify since prospects, risks, costs and consequences are usually in the hands of the technologists. In addition, this knowledge will have to be communicated in a language that general management understands.

Technologists are usually ignorant of the language general management uses, the way information is interpreted and the way the decision-making process takes place. Technologists are not usually aware of what is needed to bring new products to the market and the downstream costs associated with new product/service introduction. In addition to the downstream costs, technologists do not realize the time and costs related to developing the new capabilities needed to support the introduction of the new technology.

General managers may also be ignorant of technological developments, which makes transmission of information even more complicated. General managers may not understand the new proposed technology, and may also not understand the language associated with it.

Another issue, which complicates the communication process even further, is that needed knowledge and information is usually buffered by layers of management who do not understand technological consequences either.

In summary, while technologists are the source of technological knowledge, general managers and technologists do not speak the same language and do not have common objectives thus making the communication process difficult and the interpretation of information even harder.

Deciding on a new product/service is difficult for general managers. General managers do not fully understand the technology and do not have the knowledge to interpret the technological information. General managers are faced with taking risks on new technology developments without having a clear idea of the real costs involved.

There are three things that general managers can do to eliminate gaps between them and their firm's technologists:

1. Develop direct communication channels between general managers and their firms' technologists. This allows general managers to provide direct strategic direction and assessment of new product development. The more direct the communication channel the less likelihood for misinterpretation.

2. Establish a dual rewards system for the firm's technologists. First, rewarding the technologists for the financial contribution of the technologies to the firm's success. Second, allowing the technologists to pursue their personal research objectives.

3. Establish an education system where general managers learn the dynamics of technology and the technologists learn the dynamics profit making.

12.7 The Role of General Managers in Directing Marketing and Production for Timely Introduction of New Products/ Services to the Market

Timing of new product introduction is a major concern, since, if the firm is too early in introducing a new technology to the market, the consumers might not be ready to accept it. At the same time, if the firm is late, competition may have a first mover advantage.

When a new technology/product is invented, there are consequences for the organization's product line and profitability. The moment a new technology and its associated products are introduced to the market they displace the previous generation of products and services. Organizations phase out displaced products/ services with the associated loss in future sales of an already depreciated technology expense.

When new technologies and products are invented, general management faces a conflict between near and long-term profitability. On one hand, to maintain and increase near term profitability, it is more beneficial for a firm not to introduce a new technology and product line; but the longer the firm waits the higher the probability that its competitors will enter the market first. On the other hand, a firm has to introduce new technologies, products and services to gain long-term profitability. The decision rests in the hands of general managers to decide on the optimum timing for the introduction of new products and services to the market for maximum profitability.

In addition to future losses from not taking further advantage of an already depreciated technology, there are additional costs associated with introducing a new technology to the market. These costs are comprised of expenditures on in house support and marketing efforts for new products/services. These costs are in addition to the ones incurred to develop the new technology. Therefore, the introduction of a new product to the market is not taken lightly by general management.

There are two approaches to the innovation process and the introduction of products/services to the market: the uncontrolled and the controlled innovation processes. These processes are illustrated in Figure 12.5.

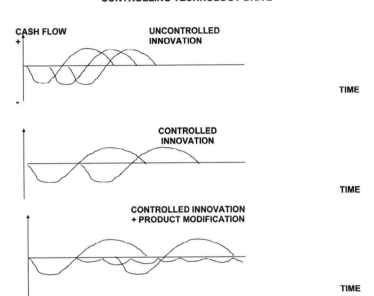

Figure 12.5
CONTROLLING TECHNOLOGY DRIVE

© H.I. Ansoff 1992

The top part of Figure 12.5 illustrates the uncontrolled innovation process where general managers have little influence in new product development with near and long-term effects in the firm's profitability.

There are certainly a number of examples of incidents where companies were either too early or too late in the introduction of a new technology/ product to the market, with direct effects on the firm's profitability. Incidents of this type have occurred in the audio industry and the digital technology when new technology and products were introduced to the market too soon.

Digital technology was invented in 1972 and CDs were first introduced to the market in the late 70's. Consumers did not react favorably to the new technology. At that time consumers were happy with LPs and 8 track tapes. CDs were again introduced to the market in the early 80's and again the consumers did not respond. Consumers were satisfied with cassette tapes. In addition, consumers found the cost of CDs too expensive since the CD players were felt to be too expensive.

When CDs were introduced again in the early 90's consumers largely embraced the "new" technology and product.

In *the controlled innovation process* general managers choose the timing of introducing new products/ services to the market.

A firm that is very successful in understanding the need of product development and its impact on market positioning is Intel. Intel develops technologies that it does not introduce when the new technologies are ready. Instead, Intel banks them; it puts them in the vault until both their customers and competitors are getting close to realizing the need and technological innovation respectively. Intel introduces new technologies based on interpretation of market needs/demand. This is certainly a risky approach but at the same time it allows Intel to maintain a technological lead while taking full advantage of market readiness.

General managers might choose to introduce new technologies to the market obsolescing their existing product line for reasons unrelated to near term profitability. This is the case of Canon, the Japanese camera manufacturer, whose general management decided to gain market share by increasing the frequency of new product introduction into the market. The goal was to gain market share by increasing the frequency of new products/ technologies introduction to the market. In the mid to late 1980s Canon introduced new products every 2.5 months with a direct impact on the firm's profitability but with a gain in market share. When the market share point advantage was attained, the frequency of new product introduction was substantially decreased.

12.8 The Role of General Managers in Choosing A Firm's Technology Strategy

In managing an organization's technology, general managers are faced with the technological and economic feasibility decisions of each project. To help determine the feasibility of these decisions, general managers utilize information from within and outside the firm. The feasibility assessment constantly influences general managers' decision to buy or develop new technologies.

There are three major areas general managers focus on while addressing issues in managing firms' technology:

1. identification of future technologies and their impact on their firm's environment,
2. assessment of the firm's internal technology capability, and,
3. integration of technology in the firm's strategy.

One of the tools general managers can use to determine a firm's future technologies is a technology surveillance system. This tool is installed in the firm to track technology developments and their impact on the firm and the firm's environment. This is accomplished by identifying and assessing trends, opportunities, discontinuities and threats of the firm's future environment.

This technological information system collects and analyses information pertinent to general managers' decision-making needs. This system also helps to determine the intensity of technology innovation and its relative importance to the firm and the firm's future technology environment.

Another area that a general manager needs to assess is the organization's internal technology capability. General managers could identify the strength of the firm's technological capability by assessing the existence of a gap between the future technology turbulence and the firm's technological capability. Based on the existence and size of gaps general management would develop action priorities.

Particularly in high technological turbulent environments, general managers need to create a flexible organization based on innovative cultures. General managers would be involved in the management of the firm's technology innovation and have expertise in technology management.

One way, which fosters technology innovation, is establishing a project management system within the firm. The project system encourages different avenues of creativity, which are then channeled into profitable development projects. The profitability estimates for each project should take into account all streams of costs, from research to market.

Another area mentioned earlier, is educating general managers and R&D managers in an effort to foster better understanding and communication between them. On one hand, general managers would be educated on the dynamics and economics of the R&D process as well as in the behaviour of creative technologists. On the other, R&D managers would be educated on strategic management decision-making process and feasibility assessment decisions.

General managers need to develop their skills in utilizing the information provided by experts when dealing with technologists in the firm and those in the technology field.

The skill of general managers in using experts is valuable both in and outside the firm. This skill entails asking experts the kinds of questions which will provide answers that general managers understand and can use in their decision making process. Honing this skill helps general managers communicate in fields where, in the majority of the times, they do not have the needed expertise.

The following are some ways to develop general managers' skills in using experts:

1. Cultivate the experts: keeping track of the outcomes predicted by the experts versus the actual outcome. This helps general managers learn the experts' bias towards higher or lower expectations.

2. Develop cross-ideological communication skills: managers and experts have norms and aspirations, which they bring to work. An understanding of these norms and their influence on experts' behaviour is helpful in evaluating the experts' proposals.

3. Use the advice of several experts: engage in discussions with different experts in the field so as to confront opinions and identify trends and technological developments.

4. Acquire sufficient knowledge in the field: managers who rely on experts should acquire sufficient knowledge about the respective fields of the experts in order to be able to judge the experts' method of analysis and its applicability to the problem to be solved.

12.9 Integration of Technology in the Firm's Strategy

There are two parts supporting the firms' future business strategy: the technology strategy and the societal strategy. Integration of these strategies is illustrated in Figure 12.6.

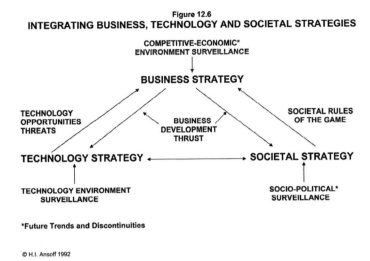

Figure 12.6
INTEGRATING BUSINESS, TECHNOLOGY AND SOCIETAL STRATEGIES

*Future Trends and Discontinuities

© H.I. Ansoff 1992

A major component of this integration is the installation of a surveillance system. This system collects information pertinent to the firm's strategic, technological and societal needs. Based on this information, general managers decide on the types of technologies to explore in the development of future projects.

Technology decisions go hand in hand with an organization's societal strategy. Firms must be aware of changes in the socio-political environment and recognize how the 'rules of the game' will impact the firm's future behaviour. Societal changes influence both the speed and impact of new technology introduction on the society. The societal changes in turn influence the firm's development of technology.

A firm's future technology is a decisive factor on its future survival. Future trends, opportunities and threats are translated into decisions on:

1. technology substitution: whether to foster extension or invention of new technologies, and

2. technology acquisition: whether to buy or develop the next-generation of technology.

General managers are constantly faced with the techno-economic decision for every project and its effects on the organization's profitability.

General managers are responsible to the firm's investors to provide an acceptable return on their investment. Usually, investors are interested in the near term profitability of the firm as measured by quarterly performance. Investment in technology is often translated into a short-term decrease in profits. Investors are resistant to a decrease in profits, but without investment in technology future profitability is threatened.

General managers are faced with the challenge of trying to find the optimal investment decision balancing between near term profitability and medium to long-term investments in technology.

In turbulent environments, general managers who are directly involved in business strategy development are more successful than those who let the firm's strategists propose future plans. The signs are that the successful organizations in the 21st century will depend on technology. As a result, technology strategy becomes an important component in the job of the general manager.

OVERVIEW

Chapters 1-5 of this book focus on the job of general management during the last half of the 20th century. An important finding of the section is that during the 21st century, it is dangerous to offer universal prescriptions for management success. The environment of the firm has become differentiated into distinctive sub-environments, each of which requires a different response.

A second important finding is that the business environment has become changeable, which makes it dangerous to make future plans by extrapolating historical successes into the future.

As a result, firms that want to stay in the competitive race must diagnose the characteristics of their future environment(s), determine the characteristics of management that will be required for success, and compare them to the present characteristics of the firm.

Chapter 6 describes the strategic diagnosis process that enables management to identify the gap between the organization's strategy and capability, and the organization's external environment. The diagnosis is based on an empirically proven Strategic Success Paradigm, which states that: "an organization will be successful if its internal capability matches its strategic response to the environment, and capability and strategy match the level of turbulence in the environment".

The strategic diagnosis identifies the type of management capability the firm must build and the type of strategic response it must develop.

Chapter 7 describes capability profiles for each level of turbulence of the firm's environment. The profiles identify the personal characteristics of the key general managers, the climate of the management organization, the competence of the organization and its capacity.

An important finding is that different turbulence levels require very different types of key managers, and the ability to manage a given turbulence level is a much more important determinant of a general manager's success than his/her knowledge of the internal workings of the firm.

Another important finding is that general managers are likely to be ineffective unless supported by an organizational climate, competence and capability which are appropriate to the environmental turbulence level.

Strategic response is discussed in Chapter 8. The focus is on responding to turbulence environments, because it is in such environments that the strategic response becomes complex and time intensive.

Two types of strategic response are discussed: positioning response, which anticipates future prospects and preplans a firm's strategic behaviour, and real time response which anticipates and responds to future threats and opportunities as they surface on the firm's horizon.

A modern positioning method called strategic posture planning is briefly described. The approach starts by segmenting the firm's environment into segments called Strategic Business Areas (SBAs), which are expected to be on different levels of turbulence and require different success behaviors.

A competitive analysis is performed on each SBA to determine the competitive position which the firm will seek in the SBA. The posture consists of the *competitive strategy, functional capability,* which supports the strategy, and *strategic investment,* which the firm will make into the SBA.

Chapter 9 focuses on strategic response at the corporate level, where the combination of competitive postures constitutes the firm's portfolio posture. Three methods, observable in current practice, of combining the competitive postures, are described: management by exception, portfolio balancing, and portfolio optimization. Each is appropriate to a different level of turbulence and different style of general management.

An important finding is that success of a firm is endangered if the style of general management leads it to select a portfolio management approach which is not responsible to the environmental imperatives.

The portfolio optimization method is described in some detail. It aims at developing a portfolio posture that meets the overall objectives and goals of the firm.

The optimization process is made difficult by the fact that in turbulent environments, a firm must pursue several objectives, which are in conflict with one another, and the goals for each objective are not comparable to one another.

These conflicts make it difficult to use a traditional method of managerial problem solving in which staff prepares recommendations and the general managers choose one of the recommended alternatives. This section describes an alternative method, which involves general managers and staff in an interactive step-by-step feedback controlled selection of the preferred portfolio posture.

Chapter 10 describes three methods for real time management: strategic issue management, which responds to fully predictable threats and opportunities, weak signal management, which responds to partially predictable threats/opportunities, and surprise management, which responds to strategic surprises.

Discussion of management capability, of competitive and portfolio postures, and real time management system completes our description of the decision making which is involved in choosing a firm's strategic response in turbulent environments.

Chapter 11 is a discussion of strategic implementation. Strategic implementation is different from implementation of annual operating plans of the firm because it encounters organizational resistance to change.

The causes of resistance are:
- strategic myopia by key general managers, which prevents the change from being implemented,
- lack of organizational capacity to handle the additional workload imposed by the change,
- incompetence of the existing systems and structures in handling the workload,
- fears and concerns by individuals that they will be unable to cope with the change,
- fears by groups and individuals of loss of power and rewards which will result from the change.

Approaches are described for dealing with respective sources of resistance. The amount of resistance that will be encountered is proportional to the gap between the management capability profile after the change, and the capability profile before the change. The resistance encountered at any point in time is inversely proportional to the time period over which the change is spread.

The period of time available to complete the change is determined by the dynamics of the market place. Therefore, the general management task is to plan the change process not to exceed the available time, to apply resistance eliminating measures early in the process, and to marshal and apply the necessary power to overcome the residual resistance.

The accordion method is introduced describing a change process that can be used during a medium urgency response. There is also a discussion on the "champion" of transformational change, the Intrapreneur.

Chapter 12 deals with the strategic management of technology, an area that needs special attention in high levels of turbulence. It addresses the communication and different views of reality between general managers and the organization's technologists.

This book outlines a strategic management system for turbulent environments. The system consists of: strategic diagnosis, designing capability, planning the firm's strategic response, implementing and controlling the implementation of the plans. A schematic flow chart of the Strategic Management System is shown in Figure 0.1.

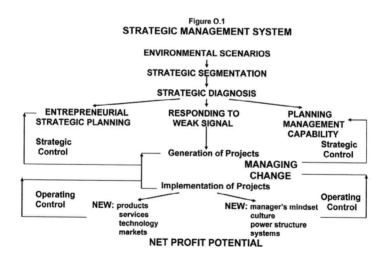

Figure 0.1
STRATEGIC MANAGEMENT SYSTEM

APPENDICES

A. GLOSSARY

ACCORDION METHOD: A method for managing change in which planning and implementation are conducted in parallel, and the duration of the change is expanded or contracted according to the urgency of the challenge.

CASH COW: An SBA in which the firm minimizes investment and maximizes cash flow to other SBAs.

COMPETITIVE POSITION: Profitability of the firm in an SBA relative to the most successful competitors.

COMPETITIVE POSTURE: The combination of the competitive strategy, capability, and strategic investment that a firm commits to an SBA.

COMPETITIVE STRATEGY: A Firm's strategy in an SBA.

CRITICAL MASS: Is the level of strategic investment in an SBA which results in profitability.

CULTURE:
a. perception of the critical success factors shared by a unit of the firm.
b. the social norms and values which support critical success factors.

DISCONTINUITY: An event that cannot be handled by the historical capability of the firm

EXTRAPOLATED COMPETITIVE POSITION: The firm's future

competitive position in an SBU estimated on the assumption that the firm's present strategy/capability will remain unchanged.

GENERAL MANAGEMENT CAPABILITY: Is the ability of the general management to support strategic behavior of a firm.

PORTFOLIO STRATEGY: Is the strategy for development of the firm's portfolio and SBAs over time.

RESISTANCE TO CHANGE: Active and passive opposition to a change which produces cost overruns, delays, distortions, or rejection of a change; behavioral resistance to change by individuals or groups; systemic resistance to change, which is induced by lack of organizational competence or capacity for handling it.

SBA - Strategic Business Area: An area of business environment that offers a distinctive growth, profitability opportunities and requires distinctive business postures to realize this opportunity.

SBU - Strategic Business Unit: A unit of the firm which is responsible for strategic development of one or more SBAs.

STAR: An SBA which has outstanding attractiveness and in which the firm expects to have an outstanding competitive position.

STRATEGIC BEHAVIOR: Optimizer of long-term profits; change of linkage with environment; strategic planning, inventing product mix, developing technologies.

STRATEGIC MANAGEMENT SYSTEM: The combination of strategic planning, capability planning, real time response, and management of implementation (including management change); total system from perception of need for strategic change to appearance of new products/services and entry in new markets in the environment.

STRATEGIC MYOPIA: Refusal to respond to information which is different from historical information due to an extrapolated position of a model of what succeeds in the environment.

STRATEGY: Logic of evolution of firm's markets, products/services, technology.

TURBULENCE: Changeability in an environment characterized by the degree of novelty challenges and the speed with which they develop
- Negative: Turbulence that poses threats to the firm.
- Positive: Turbulence that presents opportunities to the firm

TURBULENCE LEVEL: A combined measure of the degree of novelty of challenges and their speed relative to the response time of firms.

WILDCAT: An SBA that is perceived to have a potential which may vary from very profitable to a very significant loss.

REFERENCES

Ansoff, H. Igor. 1965. Corporate Strategy. New York McGraw-Hill.

Ansoff, H. Igor. 1972. "The Concept of Strategic Management." The Journal of Business Policy. (Summer). Vol. 2, No. 4.

Ansoff, H. Igor. 1979. Strategic Management. London: The MacMillan Press Ltd

Ansoff, H. Igor. 1984. Implanting Strategic Management. London: Prentice Hall International.

Ansoff, H. Igor & McDonnell, E. 1992. Implanting Strategic Management. London: Prentice Hall International.

Ansoff, H. Igor. 1986. "Competitive Strategy Analysis on the Personal Computer." Journal of Business Strategy. (Winter), Vol. 6, No. 3, pp. 28-37.

Ansoff, H. Igor, and Patrick A. Sullivan. 1989. "Competitiveness Through Strategic Behavior." Making Organization More Competitive, San Francisco Jossey-Bass, Fall.

Bell, Daniel. The Coming of Post-industrial Society: A Venture In Social Forecasting. New York, N.Y.: Basic Books.

Drucker, Peter. 1980. Managing In Turbulent Times. London: Heinemann.

Geus, Arie P. De. 1988. "Planning as Learning." Harvard Business Review, (March-April). Vol. 66, No. w: 70-74.

Lawrence, Peter. 1969. Peter Principle. New York: Morrow.

Mintzberg, Henry. 1983. Structure in Fives: Designing Effective Organizations, Englewood Cliffs, N. J.: Prentice Hall.

Parkinson, Cyril Northcote. 1957. Parkinson's Law. Boston: Houghton Mifflin

Peters, Thomas J., and Robert K Waterman. 1982. In Search of Excellence New York: Harper & Row, Publishers, Inc.

Quinn, Brian. 1980. Strategies for Change: Logical Incrementalism. Homewood: Irwin Inc.

Sanger, David E. 1988. "I.B.M. Forms 5 Autonomous Units." The New York Times, Jan. 29, p. 17.

Toffler, Alvin. 1971. The Future Shock. New York: Bantam Books.

STUDIES
EMPIRICALLY SUPPORTING THE FINDINGS

All research was conducted
at
The Ansoff Strategic Management School
U.S. International University/Alliant International University

Abu-Rahma, Ali Mohamed. 1999. "The Relationships Among National Culture, Strategic Aggressiveness, Capability and Financial Performance: The Case of Banks in Jordan and the United States".

Achua, Christopher Fru. 1992. "Relationship Between Selected Strategic Projects
Management. Factors and Performance of Project Groups of Manufacturing and/or Service Business".

Al-Hardamy, Ahmed M. 1992. "General Mangers' Personality Characteristics and
Perceptions of Environmental Turbulence as Related- to Rationality of Strategic Choice in Small Firms".

Chabane, Hassane. 1987. "Restructuring and Performance in Algerian State-Owned Enterprises: A Strategic Management Study".

Chartier, Charles. 1988. "Strategic Leadership: Product and Technology Innovations in High-Technology Companies".

Chafie, Mamdouh. 1992. "The Relationships Between Top Management Information System Profiles, Managerial Capability, and Environmental Turbulence".

Choi, Dae-Ryong. 1993. "The Relationships Between Strategic

Factors and Performance of Diversified Firms and Their Strategic Business Units in Japan".

Coop, Lind-William. 1999. "The Relationship Between Decision Style and Power Source Used in Decision-Making and Strategic Success in Christian Churches".

Djohar,. Setiadi. 1991. "The Relationships Between Strategic Effectiveness, Competitive Efficiency and Performance in Indonesian Firms".

Freidank, Jan. 1994. "Managing Transformational Change in German Business Firms".

Gabriel, Steven N. 1996. "An Empirical Assessment of a Predictive Theory of Resistance to Transformational Change in Environment-Serving Organizations".

Gahran, Brian H. 2003. "Expertise In Using Experts: A Study Of Manager-expert Strategic Decision Behavior".

Gustafson, Robert E. 2003. "The Relationships Among Environmental Turbulence, Strategic Behavior, Competitive (operating) Behavior, and Performance".

Gutu, Jackan M. 1989. "An Investigation of Environmental Dependence Hypothesis in State Owned Corporations (parastatals) in Kenya: A Strategic Management Perspective".

Han, Young Woo, 1999. "The Relationships Between Environmental Turbulence, Top Manager Mindset, Organizational Culture, Power and Performance in Korean Firms".

Hatziantoniou, Peter. 1986. "The Relationship of Environmental Turbulence, Corporate Strategic Profile, and Company Performance."

Jaja, Reuben M. 1989. "Technology and Banking: The Implications of Technological Change on the Financial Performance of Commercial banks".

Johannesson, Jokul. 1994. "The Relationships Between Strategic Intelligence Aggressiveness, Capability, and the Success of Strategic Intelligence Function".

Levitt, Catherine. 1997. "Acquisitions and Assimilation of Management Skills by Chinese Light Industrial Firms: Soft Technology Transfer to a Transitional Economy".

Lewis, Alfred 0. 1989. "Strategic Posture and Financial Performance of the Banking Industry in California: A Strategic Management Study".

Lombriser, Roman. 1992. "Impact of General Manager Leadership Behavior on the Success of Discontinuous Strategic Changes in Thirty Swiss Business Firms".

Ly, Randy T. 1995. "The Relationships Among Types of Information Systems, Levels of Environmental Turbulence and Performances of International Business Firms".

Mitiku, Abainesh. 1992. "The Relationships Between Strategic Factors and the Performance of State-Owned Industrial Enterprises in Ethiopia".

Moussetis, Robert C. 1996. "The Relationships Between Legitimacy Posture Rules of the Game and Performance of the Firm".

Phadungtin, Sarawut Jack. 2003. "The Relationships Among Merger Relatedness, Strategic Aggressiveness, Capability Responsiveness, and Merger Performance".

Randolph, Camelia J.C. 1993. "Perceived Impact of Different Types of European Community Regulations on Performance of Business Firms in the Netherlands".

Salameh, Tamer T. 1987. "Strategic Posture Analysis and Financial Performance of the Banking Industry in United Arab Emirates: A Strategic Management Study".

Schultze, Ralf F.P. 1994. "Differences of Corporate Management Behavior to Foster Success of Intrapreneurs in Charge of Incremental or Discontinuous Innovations".

Sullivan, Patrick A. 1987. "The Relationship Between Proportion of Income Derived from Subsidy and Strategic Performance of a Federal Agency Under the Commercial Activities Program".

Taylor, Julia. 1992. "Factors and Behaviors Associated with Successful Technology Substitution Decisions in the High Turbulence Environment".

Thabet, Saib Sallam. 1993. "The Relationship Between Strategic Choice Technology and Success of Technology Transfer to Local Firms in Less-developed Countries: The Case of Yemen".

Van der Velden, Thorsten. 1997. "The Relationships Between Corporate General Management Behavior and the Success of Strategic Portfolio Management in German Business Firms".

Thorsell, Jorgen M. 1990. "A Framework for Determination of Strategies for General Manager Transformational Development".

Valdez, Thorsel Van Der. 1997. "The Relationships Between Corporate Management Behavior and the Success of Strategic Portfolio Management in German Business Firms".

Wang, Pien. 1991. "Determinants of Perception of Environmental Turbulence and Strategic Response of Savings and Loan Top Manages".

Yum, Jihwan. 2000. "The Relationships Among Environmental Turbulence, Strategic Aggressiveness of Information Technology, Organizational Information Technology Capability, and Organizational Performance".

ANSPLAN PRODUCT LINE

ANSPLAN PRODUCT LINE

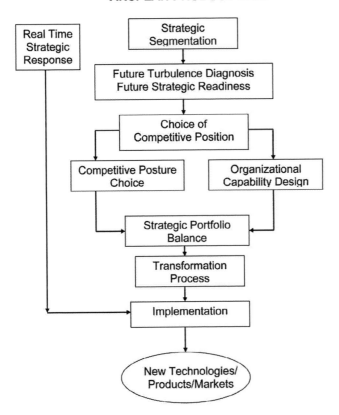

Copyright: H. Igor Ansoff 1979, 1984, 1990, 1992, 1995, 1997, 2004

ANSPLAN PRODUCT LINE - PRODUCTS

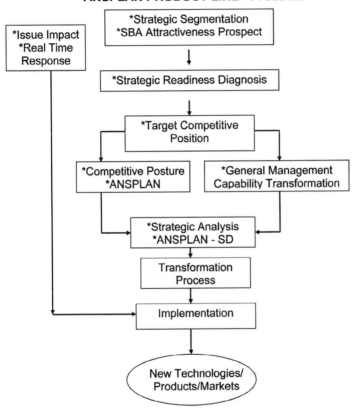

ANSPLAN PRODUCT LINE - Products

*Strategic Segmentation
*SBA Attractiveness Prospect

*Issue Impact
*Real Time Response

*Strategic Readiness Diagnosis

*Target Competitive Position

*Competitive Posture
*ANSPLAN

*General Management Capability Transformation

*Strategic Analysis
*ANSPLAN - SD

Transformation Process

Implementation

New Technologies/ Products/Markets

ANSPLAN PRODUCT LINE
List of Tools

Vision of the Future
Real Time Issue Management
Strategic Segmentation
Strategic Diagnosis
Target Competitive Position
General Management Capability Design
Change Management
Competitive Posture Analysis
Competitive Posture Analysis Data
Competitive Portfolio Optimization
Societal Strategy
Technology Management Assessment
ANSPLAN

THE ANSOFF INSTITUTE

Contact

Tel: 760 740 0258
Fax: 760 740 0259
Web Page: www.ansoff.com
Email: DrPHA@aol.com

THE ANSOFF INSTITUTE

1. Vision

2. Mission

3. Concept Introduction

4. What does The Institute do

5. Benefits to Members and Communities

6. Benefits to Participating Organizations

7. Benefits to Affiliate Academic Institutions

8. Benefits to Alumni

THE ANSOFF INSTITUTE

A registered 501(c)(3) non-for-profit organization
Tax number: 30-0032098

All donations are tax deductible

1. Vision

To be a leading research institute developing and innovating new Strategic Management technologies and translating them into practical applications.

2. Mission

To educate members and communities in the latest thinking and techniques in the field of Strategic Management.

3. Concept Introduction

- To operationalize the concept of Strategic Management from research that is being developed
  1. concept development, and
  2. applying operational theory to practical applications
- Prior research has predominantly stressed concept development. Little work has been recognized in developing workable tools and applications.

4. What does The Institute do

The Institute:

- Links Theory and Practice on all contributions in the area of strategic management
- Researches and operationalizes the findings
- Conducts applied research based on industry needs/wants
- Performs research on for-profit organizations, for not-for-profits and governmental agencies. Some of the work has been completed and some is in process. The research projects include the health care, government and charitable sectors.
- Is an incubator / think-tank for strategic thinking
- Is involved in consulting based activities by providing know how, tools and manpower support in the field of strategic management
- Works with both national and international firms in appropriate tool usage under diverse environments
- Sponsors a scholar in residence to do research in the field of strategic managements. Part of the assignment would be for the scholar to deliver the finings select lecture settings around the world. The scholar would also have to write an article to be published as well.
- Has a group of experts who would work 'on loan' for a designated amount of time to firms as consultants to assist in implementing strategies. The awardee firms will meet on an annual basis to review developments and processes. There would be selection criteria to be part of this group.
- Recognizes individuals as well as organizations who have made significant contribution in the field

Individuals:

Managers who have applied the concepts

- Nomination on a region or country basis
- Invite to speak about the intervention
- Levels of recognition

Academics who have invented or written concepts

- Global nomination

   Organizations:

- Ones which applied the concepts

Nomination on a region or country basis to further recognize

   Academic: Institutions which teach and practice the concepts

Students: University level - nominated by the lead professor
          Dissertation award
- Provides Certification in the field of strategic management. Develop an acronym to be added at the end of ones name after they pass an exam or reach a level of competence; become a recognized specialist in the field.

The findings are communicated to the communities by:
- Creating or cooperating with a Journal to publish research
- Writing Essays and Monographs to communicate findings
- Developing a Compendium of findings
- Establishing a Data base for collaborative research
- Holding an annual Conference 1.5 days
- Offering trained Interns
- Conducting and presenting the findings of validated empirical research

The purpose of the Institute is to transfer and communicate strategic research to practical applications

5. Benefits to Members and Communities

- Hold regular meetings for planners and upper level management. The emphasis of these events will be to introduce the latest information, applications, tools in the strategic management area by experts in the field.
- Publish newsletter with latest information which would include:
- Profile of members and their achievements
- Summaries of research, needs achievements and other information

6. Benefits to Participating Organizations

- Access to Institute's resources to solve organizations' problems or issues in the area of Strategic Management
- Training ground with opportunities to participate in Workshops and Seminars while obtaining certificates, diplomas and degrees from affiliate Universities in the field of Strategic Management
- Research, tools and applications designed to solve organizations' needs
- Faculty access and support
- Incubator of research

Research based applications and methodology
- Data bank
- Design tools and applications
- Access to trained interns available to work on assignments
- Research monographs or applied research
- Priority recruitment of Strategic Management graduates from the master and doctoral studies
- Name recognition

7. Benefits to Affiliate Academic Institutions

- Research
- Access to pool of students for joint research
- Access to pool of organizations for research and joint assignments
- Research collaboration
- Share in contracted research
- Training and workshops
- Articles and publications
- Faculty exchanges as visiting professors
- Strategic Management student exchanges
- Affiliation and recognition

8. Benefits to Alumni

All Strategic Management students at affiliated universities automatically become life members of the Institute. The Doctoral graduates hold a separate Advisory designation which include the following benefits:

Personal
- Perpetuity of Ansoff's name and research in the field
- Access to updated research material
- Receive newsletter and updates on the Institute
- Improved visibility of affiliate universities' Strategic Management Program

Professional
- All of the benefits enjoyed by Participating and Sponsor organizations

Contact

The Ansoff Institute
2166 Lemon Avenue
Escondido, CA 92029

Tel: 760 740 0258
Fax: 760 740 0259
www.ansoff.com

OPEN COMPANY, LTD

In a complex global environment that is more turbulent because of the increasing speed of change, unpredictability of outcomes, novelty of challenges, discontinuous trends and instability of key success factors, our clients are looking for a trusted partner in innovation, growth and renewal, globally.

OPEN Company, Ltd

We enable leaders' growth in exploring and creating a better future.

OPEN Company's focus is on improving the long-term profitability of our client by synchronizing internal structure, operation and strategy with external market requirements. The results are created by our unique way of working, where we act as a catalyst and provide support throughout the internal change process.

OPEN's approach is based upon recognized, proven methodologies that lead to efficient solutions, adapted to each client's unique situation. Involvement, participation and ownership of the new solutions throughout the organization, from the co-workers to top management, are the essential ingredients for our work and success of our engagements.

OPEN is able to deliver on this promise by providing knowledge transfer together with process coaching in Strategic and Operational Excellence as well as Excellence in leadership. Process coaching is a set of activities on the part of the coach that help the client visualize, understand, and act upon the process events that occur in the client's environment in order to improve the situation as defined by the client.

OPEN is a headquartered in London, United Kingdom, with offices in **Copenhagen, Denmark; Oslo, Norway; San Diego, California; Santiago, Chile; Stockholm, Sweden; and Warsaw, Poland**. We work with companies of all sizes, small to Global 1000 in a variety of industries such as telecom, pharma and biotech, manufacturing, IT, transportation and financial services.

Our invitation to explore the future today

www.opencompany.net.